# Job Interview

The Quick and Complete Guide to Winning an Interview

(Self Help Guide to Land the Job in Start-ups)

**Gayle Ryan**

Published by Rob Miles

**Gayle Ryan**

All Rights Reserved

*Job Interview: The Quick and Complete Guide to Winning an Interview (Self Help Guide to Land the Job in Start-ups)*

ISBN 978-1-989990-62-9

All rights reserved. No part of this guide may be reproduced in any form without permission in writing from the publisher except in the case of brief quotations embodied in critical articles or reviews.

Legal & Disclaimer

The information contained in this book is not designed to replace or take the place of any form of medicine or professional medical advice. The information in this book has been provided for educational and entertainment purposes only.

The information contained in this book has been compiled from sources deemed reliable, and it is accurate to the best of the Author's knowledge; however, the Author cannot guarantee its accuracy and validity and cannot be held liable for any errors or omissions. Changes are periodically made to this book. You must consult your doctor or get professional medical advice before using any of the suggested remedies, techniques, or information in this book.

Upon using the information contained in this book, you agree to hold harmless the Author from and against any damages, costs, and expenses, including any legal fees potentially resulting from the application of any of the information provided by this guide. This disclaimer applies to any damages or injury caused by the use and application, whether directly or indirectly, of any advice or information presented, whether for breach of contract, tort, negligence, personal injury, criminal intent, or under any other cause of action.

You agree to accept all risks of using the information presented inside this book. You need to consult a professional medical practitioner in order to ensure you are both able and healthy enough to participate in this program.

# Table of Contents

INTRODUCTION .................................................................. 1

CHAPTER 1: RESEARCHING PHASE ..................................... 5

CHAPTER 2: A SWEATY FOREHEAD!! BREATHLESSNESS!! A SORT OF A RESTLESS FEELING!! ........................................ 10

CHAPTER 3: CAREER PATH ................................................ 32

CHAPTER 4: WHY THIS IS IMPORTANT ............................. 37

CHAPTER 5: INITIAL INTRODUCTIONS .............................. 48

CHAPTER 6: TOP JOB INTERVIEW QUESTIONS ................ 52

CHAPTER 7: THE BIG QUESTION: WHAT QUALITIES ARE INTERVIEWERS LOOKING FOR? ........................................ 68

CHAPTER 8: USEFUL WAYS YOU CAN IMPRESS YOUR INTERVIEWER .................................................................. 76

CHAPTER 9: YOUR FEARS .................................................. 90

CHAPTER 10: MAINTAINING RAPPORT AND RESPECT .... 106

CHAPTER 11: THINGS YOU SHOULD AVOID IN A JOB INTERVIEW ..................................................................... 111

CHAPTER 12: PREPARATION ........................................... 117

CHAPTER 13: PASS WITH FLYING COLORS ..................... 122

CHAPTER 14: THE NEXT STEP ......................................... 137

CHAPTER 15: WHY DO YOU WANT THIS JOB? ................ 152

**CHAPTER 16: DURING THE INTERVIEW: COMMON QUESTIONS PART 1** ...................................................... **167**

**CHAPTER 17: THE PHONE RINGS** ................................... **177**

**CONCLUSION** .............................................................. **182**

## Introduction

This book contains proven steps and strategies on how to ace job interviews. Sounds simple, doesn't it? The chances are you have tried your own little search for acing job interviews online- and let's face it there is a plethora of information available out there. From standard questions to sample answers and dress codes; it is all pretty basic and easy to understand.

But even with ALL that information on how to prepare for job interviews out there AND available for free, the interview-to-hire ratio still remains quite unimpressive. According to a survey report by the recruiting software company Lever, an average of 1 in 100 candidates is hired. For a hundred people going through all that 'information' available online, only one person makes it. Do you think that only one of those one hundred candidates are educated enough or experienced enough for that job? Most likely not. Was he the only one who checked up on how to answer the esteemed 'tell us about yourself' question? Arguably not. But out of those hundred, there was only one who was prepared for more than just the template version of giving a job interview. The fact is, recruiters are trained to screen candidates by holding a conversation with them. Employees are any organizations greatest asset and the most costly. Labor costs can add up to 70% of the total costs of running a business, according to Paycor. Organizations know this, and they want to make sure that they hire people that will make up for that expense. And while education and experience are important, they need to know that a candidate will fit in the organization, understand their values, goals, and culture and be willing to embody it. Job interviews are designed to understand all this and more about a certain candidate- understand more about you. If you believe template answers and a tailored blazer would make the cut, then you may want to think again before you encounter any more interview failures. And this is exactly where this book comes in. This book is designed to help you better understand your strengths and weaknesses so that you can aptly communicate the same to your interviewers.

This book highlights the importance of using the right words and structuring the right sentences to communicate your experiences aptly. Did you know you actually speak on an average of 100 words per minute while you think about 900? More often than not, a lot of important information is lost in translation. In your head, you may have great ideas and ambitions for your prospective job, but you may not be able to communicate them?

This book also highlights tips and tactics to communicate better and also listen to the unsaid. To actually read between the lines of what the interviewer is asking and what is he expecting to learn from your answers.

You know the top questions most

interviewers ask, but do you know WHY they ask them? These standard questions are designed to tap into specific aspects of your education, experience and work ethics; and by understanding the reasons behind these questions; you will get a better idea of how to answer them. All in all, this book is designed to answer all your job interview queries and apprehensions to help you stand out among 100 other candidates, but any other number of candidates by simply understanding your recruiters' objectives and your own strengths. Better get started, right?

**Chapter 1: Researching Phase**

Before you even get started on preparing for the kind of questions that might get asked, you need to first have a solid understanding of the company you are applying to. For example, you need find out the type of interview format or the financial state of the company. Doing research on the company will prepare you and give you a sense of what to expect on the actual interview day. It would also help you to understand if this company is really one that you want to invest your time and energy in.

One of the biggest mistakes in preparing for an interview is not researching about the company as a whole. Interviewers like to ask questions about the company's general information because it lets them gauge if you are truly interested and passionate about coming aboard. Being able to score in this section is crucial in convincing the interviewer that you are serious about taking on this role you are applying to.

So how should you prepare for this? Well, the fortunate truth is – even if you've previously never heard of the company you're interviewing with, you can still walk in like you've known about the place for years. Here are 3 ways to tackle researching the company pre-interview:

1) Know the Strength – Knowing the strength and competitive edge of the company is a great way to convince your interviewer that you have done a thorough research. It shows that you value the company high enough to have spent the effort and time to find out more. This information can usually be found through a simple Google search or on the company websites themselves. Companies also share how they stand out in the market through their mission or values, which are typically prominently displayed in the "About Us" section.

2) Financial Health – You want to join a company that is doing great in its finances (unless you like the thrill of living on the edge and not knowing when you might get retrenched). Getting employed in a well off company also mean that you will not miss your regular bonuses and benefits as an employee. For most large companies, you should be able to access and listen to publicly available earnings report. These reports will talk about the outlook of the company, latest product information as well as the revenue generated. If you are interviewing for a start up, you can gauge the prospects of it by looking at the amount of funding it has received or looking through its press releases. Crunchbase.com is a good resource to start looking. Once you have this information, you can make your own judgements. While you don't necessarily have to talk about the financial state of the company in the interview, being able to talk about the relevant subjects backed up with financial facts is impressive to the hiring manager.

3) Company Culture – Understanding the company culture is important because you want to make sure that you are a good fit for the company. Nothing is worse than coming to work on the first day and find that you dread the working environment and facing your colleagues. To find out more about the company's culture, you can look up the company's blog or social media accounts. Understanding this information will also help you decide which topics to talk about during the interview and which ones you should not bring up. For example, if the company culture is about pursuing excellence through hard work, you might not want to bring up the topic of work-life balance until you at least get the offer.

Besides researching about company information, you should also find out what format of interview does the company conduct so that you can better prepare yourself. Is it a one-to-one interview, multiple-to-one interview or perhaps even a group interview? Is it a case study interview or regular question-and-answer interview? These are just some of the questions you should have answers to before you attend the interview. You should strategize your interview based on the format of the interview conducted. For example, if it's a case study interview, you might want to look up case study examples and research on the best way to answer a case study question.

With that said, while it is important to find out everything about the company you are applying to, it is also equally critical that you assess your own skills and expertise so that you can play to your strength on the big day.

## Chapter 2: A Sweaty Forehead!! Breathlessness!! A Sort Of A Restless Feeling!!

Have you ever gone through such experiences, just before the night of an interview? Or finally when your name is called out to proceed towards the room and in such situations, you always loose your confidence. Isn't it?

Many candidates who want to appear for an interview wish there was a way to get a job without having an interview for it. Interview setup makes them insanely nervous, to the point where they can't even get to sleep the night before an interview. This is called Interview-Fear or phobia.

Before detailing any useful tips for interview preparation, let me explain you that one has to come out of that fear first. Overcoming your interview-fear will not only make you confident to sit in front of the interviewer but also raise the probability of getting selected.

You prepare for your interview. You prepare like crazy. You spend hours and hours researching the company and rehearsing your answers you're going to answer in. Sometimes you just hate walking into an interview room, facing the panel and trying to answer questions. Sometimes you can't put your thoughts in order and henceforth you fail in your interview.

To overcome all the fears, one has to understand that the H.R. / interviewer is also a human being like you. Remember, he/she must have also sat on your chair once after their graduation, for a job. You can relax yourself by taking the viewpoint - This is just a conversation about one of my favorite topics: "The work I do."

**THINK:**

"I like my work and I do enjoy talking about it. If the person who's interviewing me today likes my passion for music that's great. If they don't like my passion for music that's fine too. I only want to work with people who resound at my frequency. I don't have anything to prove today."

Most job-seekers worry about interviews because they truly believe that every interview is a precious opportunity not to be wasted. They go to every interview thinking "Please God, don't let me down this time!"

That's too much pressure to put on yourself. Nobody can please everyone. You will delight some interviewers and turn off others. So what? If somebody doesn't like you that's their problem, not yours.

Here are few suggestions to break the barrier of fear. You just need to understand;

What's the worst that can happen? Try to imagine what would be the worst possible outcome of your interview-fears and write it down.

Control your Imagination. Don't start imagining negative just out of your fear. Stop assumptions.

Breathe through your fears and meditate.

Here are a few collection of questions (along with the purpose) which H.R. Deptt mostly asks.

Question: Tell us something about yourself.

(This usually is a question to start the communication and set the ball rolling for the interview.)

The trick is to put the full stop at the right place to provoke the next question you want.

For e.g. "last month I developed an android app on Google playstore. Though it was challenging but an interesting task which I thoroughly enjoyed."

Question: Why do you consider yourself a suitable candidate for this position?

The answer to this question lies in the preparation you did before the interview. It is very important that you research the requirements of the position well and further match them with your skills.

Question: What do you know about us?

Research the company and its business a bit before appearing for the interview. Also, find out a bit about the technologies they work upon.

For e.g. I see that your company does a lot of projects based on Open Source platforms like Linux Kernel, MySQL which is quite interesting as I have a similar kind of experience.

NOTE: I strongly recommend to simply go to the company website, glance at their LinkedIn page. That's all it takes!

Here's some more information you can look for:

What do they sell?

How many employees do they have?

Who is the CEO?

When were they founded?

What are they best known for?

These are just a few examples. You can research other areas too. You just need a couple of facts you can answer when they ask this question.

Just show them you read about them and know the company you're interviewing with.

Question: What do you do to improve your knowledge?

The field of IT is very revolutionary. I keep myself updated with latest technologies.

I'm an active member of some IT Groups on LinkedIn which keeps me updated with upcoming technological developments. I take some time out of my work schedule so that I can keep sharpening my saw.

Question: Can you perform under pressure?

(Expect pressure in everything you do. It is important to maintain your performance and develop strategies to deliver under pressure. You can then go ahead and talk about your way of dealing with pressure and performing under it.)

Working well under pressure is a good strength to have. But saying yes is not enough; you need to explain how you can handle pressure situation to bring the best out of it. Tell the interviewer that you work the same with pressure and without pressure.

For e.g. I try to react on situations, rather than on stress. That way, the situation is handled and doesn't become stressful at all.

For e.g. I enjoy working under pressure because I believe it helps me in growing. In my previous experience, while handling my major projects during the final year of graduation, I worked well during deadlines, and I always learned how to work more efficiently afterwards.

For e.g. I work well under pressure because I don't get panic and take it as a challenge. I maintain self control and work as efficiently as possible.

Question: Discuss the most stressful situation you came across in your previous job.

Here you should discuss a stressful situation that you were able to overcome and keep a positive tone, do not say you never came across a stressful situation.

Typical answers can be:

In my previous job, our team's targets were just doubled along with the incentives, initially everyone was happy by the number, but we discussed it with our project manager and he was matured enough to understand the situation. But he wanted us to give it a try and was ready to reduce the targets to a more realistic number.

You can also talk about a very significant project where you worked for long hours or may be in double shifts and had to sacrifice on family time, but once the project was done you got recognition for the hard work and you were over the stress.

Question: Tell us some of your strengths.

Again, it is important to study the requirements of the position before you appear for the interview. Roll out your strengths and offer the ones that the post demands.

Question: Tell us some of your weaknesses.

Every human being has weaknesses, so it is perfectly OK for you to have some too.

The right way to answer will be to turn one of your strengths as a weakness, portray your strength as weakness and say that others accuse you of having this weakness but you think it is important to work in this manner.

Question: Are you comfortable working in a team?

Be it an IT company, an industry, or a corporate office, the whole work is a team work. So, your answer to this question should be: "Yes, I am comfortable working in a team."

NOTE: However, if you have any problem in working as a team, it is better to work on those problems and develop yourself as a team player.

Question: How do you rate your communication skills?

Good communication skills mean, the ability to understand and explain in a common language.

So, if you believe that your communication skills are weaker, you need to work on them.

NOTE: Anything less than average or good is not acceptable in the interview.

Question: You do not have all the experience we need for this position!

**RELAX!** An interviewer will rarely ask this question as they usually scan your profiles before they call for an interview. If they still ask this question, they only want to judge how well can you adapt to negativity.

Your answer can be:

"I may not have all the experience required for the role. However, we all start from scratch level. And it's not about how much I know, it's about how much I can learn here in your esteemed company. I have a passion to learn and I'm sure I will do it sir".

Also, if you meet most of the requirements, you can say that, "Sir, as you can see, I possess most of the qualities needed for this role and for the remaining I'm always open to learning them."

NOTE: Stay confident while answering this question.

Question: How would you compensate for the lack of experience you have for this position?

As we discussed in the previous question, your ability to understand and pick up new things quickly should be able to compensate for the lack of work experience you have.

Question: If you were hiring for this position, what qualities would you look for in a potential candidate?

Closely understand the qualities and skills a person holding the position would need and match them with the qualities you possess.

Question: Do you know anyone who works for us?

Offer some one's name only if they really know you well and can offer a positive feedback about you.

Question: What is your style of management?

In current scenario, everything is customized. We need tailor-made solutions. Today, one size can't fit to all. That is, one management style won't work in all the situations. So, better offer "situational" as your style of management.

Question: How would you go about firing a person, if required?

The basic purpose of asking this question is to check your EQ (Emotional Quotient) and see if you have the guts to make hard decisions. Tell that you would try to do your best to ensure that your team members perform to its best but if any particular member is not able to perform even after taking all the necessary steps by you to help him, you would make the hard decision to ensure that the assignment/work doesn't suffer.

Question: Is there any particular kind of person you can not work with?

The answer to this question should be a "No". This is basically a different way of putting up the question to know your compatibility level.

Question: What qualities would you look for in your senior?

Mention some generic qualities like intelligence, good sense of humor, dedicated to his team, leadership qualities, go-getter etc.

Question: What motivates you at work?

To answer this question, you can mention few things (depending upon you) like- the new challenges in the work, learning new things, good management, healthy working environment, mentoring and coaching others, meeting deadlines/targets etc.

Question: Will you be happy to work in night shifts or over the weekends?

You need to answer this question taking into consideration what is suitable for you. Say you can work in the night shifts, only if you can really do it. Else, take an excuse on it.

Question: Have you ever committed a mistake at work?

To err is human.

There's no harm to accept, if you committed a mistake at work but before answering the question re-analyze the gravity of mistake you made. What actually more important is:-

Question: What did you do to rectify the mistake and make sure that you don't do it again?

So, mention the mistake you committed and keep the 'focus of the answer' on the measurements you took to rectify it.

Question: What position would you prefer while working on a project?

Basically, this question is for you to answer based on the skills and qualities you possess. If you have the capability to handle different positions, you may discuss that also in the interview.

Question: What are the most important things for you as a manager?

The two things which should be most important for a manager to succeed in his/her role are:

His/her team should always be happy at work and should keep high performing.

The assignment/project he/she is working on with his/her team is successfully finished with minimal problems.

Question: Will you be happy to re-locate, if required?

Answering such questions are totally dependent on your position. If you are entertaining this question in the interview, it is better to discuss this with your family prior before you go to face the interview.

Question: What kind of a salary are you looking for?

This is bit tricky question. Here you can try to put the ball back in the HR's court by asking him about what salary they offer for a position like this. (Remember, most of the reputed companies have a fixed remuneration at each level.)

But being a fresher, most of the times you will have to accept the company's offering for the position. However, if the salary offered is below your expectations, you can definitely discuss that during the interview.

Question: For how long do you expect to stay with our organization?

You should ensure that you give an impression that you will pay back more than what you take from the company:

You can say, "I will stay here as far as I see an opportunity for growth, as I am looking for a stability in work place."

If they stress on number of years say, "3-4 years, and more if I can explore new challenges/growth opportunities."

Question: Why should we hire you?

Here you should discuss the position/post you have applied for and your strengths/experiences with which you can add value to the applied job.

Also, discuss the achievements of your previous job (if you had any), and say that I have developed my skills to suit my current profile, but I want to develop myself further and face new challenges, and for that I need to change my job.

You may also add by saying that you will always be willing to take charge and responsibilities to suit company requirements.

Question: What is your idea of an ideal company?

Do not go to extreme, it might give an impression to the interviewer that you are very demanding.

You may say;

How far an ideal company is concern, I believe an ideal company provides maximum opportunities for growth of their employees.

An ideal company will provide comfortable and flexible working environment, so that their employees can perform maximum and work for company's vision.

A company that encourages learning OR in 3T (Train The Trainers)

Question: Tell us something about your achievements at your previous job.

Talk about your professional achievements scored/earned in your previous job, like, you were recognized as a "High-Performer of the Month" OR probably you get an "Appreciation Letter" from the company or client. Any good feedback from your manager in the previous job.

You can also discuss your annual ratings. Do not forget to discuss your promotions/appraisals (if any) in your previous job.

Question: Discuss your 5 characteristics.

List down points that will help you professionally:

Independent

Responsible

Hard working

Multi-tasker

Prompt

You may add your own characteristics in the list.

NOTE: Answer it with honesty, as they can go deeper into this discussion.

Question: Tell us something about your hobbies.

You can include:

Surfing internet,

Blogging,
Listening music,

Reading books,

Playing cricket,

and so on…

NOTE: Answer it with honesty, as they can go deeper into this discussion.

Question: What is more important to you, money or success?

(This is tricky question, as money and success both are important and you cannot overlook the importance of one over the other.)

You can say, "Sir, How far money and success are concerned, I would say, both are important for me, but if I have to choose one out of two, definitely I will choose success. The reason being, if I will be successful, money will automatically follow."

Question: Do you have any questions for us?

Generally, this is the last question expected during an interview.

Research the company a bit and discuss if they have been in news recently. You can also discuss about the growth prospects for you within the company etc.

## Chapter 3: Career Path

A graduate who goes in search of an employment is expected to have generic skills. These are described as basic skills like communication, reading and working knowledge. A specialised skill in the area of study or the role will be called domain skill. After gathering experience when he goes to higher level, he would need Transformational skill.

What are the reasons for not getting a job?

Call them if you don't get a call within a given time frame and don't forget to write a thank you letter to an organization for taking out their precious time for your interview. Few reasons for not getting a job:

- Lack of communication skills, written or oral

- Inappropriate attitude could have pulled down

- Lack of knowledge about the working world
- Lack of confidence
- Inappropriate/fake degree
- Lack of experience
- Lack of motivation

Once a candidate gets selected in his first job, he has to strive hard for upward mobility. He should not conclude to rest at that stage for ever. He has to keep moving to higher levels of management with leadership skills. He has to take interest in knowing about what is happening in other departments of the organisation. Many top level managers might not get to know data on capital investment and expenses, wealth management, accounting pattern, sales turnover, manpower planning, fund flow and share value.

Invariably it is seen that every eight out of ten (8/10) among corporate executives are from the background of finance and marketing. Those from other streams of management inching to top are very low. It is the competence that drives to know about the general administration and running of the organisation and its group. A focus on short term performance is fine but it is also important to view at long term business leadership.

What it takes to be a CEO?

Forbes came out with a neat survey on the study of CEO, CMO and CTO characteristics. Traditional CEOs came from anyplace but marketing. Companies that focussed more on operational excellence looked to their finance teams for filling up the top seat. Organizations focused on innovation might look to a CTO type.

Those focussing on market share concentrated on sales guys. Such organizations mainly focused on the proven dynamic relationship between clients and customers along B2B and B2C segments.

Besides competency they would need passion to be a CEO /CTO/ CMO. I list out some essential attributes of successful leaders. They are:

i)Ability to focus on the vision and communicate the vision to the stake holders.

ii)Awareness of operational details of the organisation, though they do not handle in their job role

iii)Being an avid reader on industry trends

iv)Hires strong management teams to support their decisions.

v) Articulate needs of customer, challenges and business goals.

The competencies mapped for leadership position are:

- Organisational Reporting
- Fund Management
- Customer Relationship
- Influencing Leadership skill

- Internal Control
- Communication
- Management Accounting
- Planning & Strategy
- HR System & Compliance
- Technical Competence
- Industry Knowledge

By the time he reaches the top seat, he should have acquired insight knowledge and necessary skill to execute and keep the ball rolling.

**Chapter 4: Why This Is Important**

Understanding the purpose of the job is very important to becoming a successful candidate. By understanding what the job entails you will be able to write an effective cover letter, relating your experience, education, skills and talents to the position in an attempt to convince the company that you are the right fit for the job. This is how you will land yourself an interview.

This information is also important when going into a job interview. You will need to be familiar with the position so that you are prepared to answer questions that will relate to the job. There are a myriad of questions that interviewers might ask. By knowing the purpose of the job you are better able to be prepared and anticipate what questions might be asked.

Whatever information you don't have about what the job entails you can ask during the interview. Make yourself a brief list of points about the job that need clarification. This will give you something to say when the interview asks if you have any questions, which always happens. You don't want to be left with nothing to say when this question comes up, and it always does.

Zeroing In on Your Right Job

It can be difficult to sift through all of the job postings in your area. Zeroing in on the right jobs for you to apply for can be tricky. Figuring out the purpose of the job you are looking at helps, but it isn't the only thing to consider.

Before you ever start looking for a job you need to answer some basic questions for yourself. The answers to these questions will help you determine if you should spend your time applying for a job or not. Here is a list of the questions you need to ask yourself.

What is your ideal title?

What education do you have?

How many years of experience do you have, and in what positions or industries?

What skills do you have that you can prove?

What talents do you have?

What have been your past accomplishments in your work experience?

What is the minimum hourly wage or salary you are willing to entertain?

Are you looking for a job or a career move? Do you want a company with opportunity for advancement?

Are there any companies you specifically want to work for?

Are there any companies you specifically do not want to work for?

When you have the answers to these questions mapped out it will greatly assist you in your job search. You will be able to quickly sift through jobs that do not meet your expectations.

Today, many job postings do not list the offered salary or wage. However, the applications will likely ask for your minimum wage requirements. Make sure you don't short change yourself. The company may have a budget of $15 per hour, but if you ask for $12 that is what you will get if hired. On the other hand, if your wage expectation is too high you will not get a call back from the company at all.

If you do not have the qualifications required by the job poster, you should not apply for the job. When you apply for jobs that you do not meet the qualifications for you will be wasting your time and theirs. If a position comes up later that match your qualifications, you may be denied an interview because the company remembers that you applied for a position that didn't match your qualifications, and you wasted their time.

If a job posting lists preferred qualifications that you don't meet, but you do meet the required qualifications, you can go ahead and apply for the job. Before doing so you should carefully consider why that qualification is preferred. What part of the job would this qualification relate to? Would you be able to perform the job effectively without that qualification?

With each job posting you look at, you want to look at it from both your point of view and the company's point of view. First, look at it from your angle. Does this sound like a job you would enjoy and excel at? Then look at it from the company's angle. Would they agree that you are able to perform the tasks of the job? Could you convince them to hire you? If you don't think the answer is yes, you should move on. You do not want to waste your time applying for jobs that you probably can't get.

One more thing to consider is that you want to find a job you can stick to for a long period of time. No one likes a job hopper. The more jobs you have within a year's time the harder it will be to find a new one. Make sure that whatever job you apply for is one that you know you can excel in and keep for the long term.

Finding Your Right Job

Actually performing the job search is going to be much easier once you have an idea of what job will be right for you. Performing a search will be somewhat time consuming, but will be well worth the effort.

You will want to search multiple job posting websites. Some good websites are Indeed, CareerBuilder, Monster, and Snag-a-job. Do individual searches on each of these websites. If you limit yourself to just one website you may miss open positions that are perfect for you. You don't want to miss any opportunities that could arise.

When you search these websites you will want to use the advanced search option. Your key words should be the position title or type that you are seeking. You should not put in too many keywords, however, or it will severely limit your search and you could miss positions that you could be applying for. If you have a minimum salary requirement you can put that into the search engine. To further limit your search results you can include some basic qualifications that you have, such as your level of education or years of experience.

You should also limit your search by choosing how old you want the postings to display. As a general rule you will want to look at jobs posted within the last seven days. Jobs posted a month or more ago will likely already be filled, or there will be active candidates already being interviewed. The posting likely has been neglected to be taken down when it is that old. The oldest postings you should look at are 2 weeks old.

If you enter your search criteria and do not come up with very many listings you may need to broaden your search. Sometimes job postings will not list any of this information. When you search with limitations, those job postings may be omitted. By broadening your search you will be able to look at more jobs. The downside to this is that there will be many more jobs to sift through that are obviously not the right fit for you. However, this approach could help you prevent missing opportunities for the perfect job.

As you look at each posting you should look for jobs that meet the requirements you identified when asking yourself the questions listed in the last section of this book. You should also make sure that you are qualified for the position, and that you feel you can perform the duties listed.

Do not stop there. If you are not familiar with a company you should research it briefly before applying for the job. Sometimes the company is not listed in the job posting, and you may want to go ahead and apply. If the company is listed it is beneficial to check out the company on a website such as Glass Door. This will give you an idea of what it is like to work for the company and how stable the company is. It will also give you an idea of how much promoting they do from within the company, which is also important if you are looking for a career move and not just a job to get by.

Once you are sure that you are interested in the job, you should go ahead and take the time to apply. Be certain that it is worth your time. Most positions now require an in depth application as well as some type of assessment. Even applying for fast food positions can take up to an hour or more of your time to complete the entire application process. You don't want to spend that time if you aren't sure you want the job.

How Are You Special and Unique?

In order to properly apply for a job and prepare for an interview you have to ask yourself what makes you special and unique. What qualities do you possess that make you right for this job?

This doesn't have to be all about education and work experience. What you have to offer goes far beyond this. While that may be what shows on your resume, it is not all you have to offer a company. You need to consider all of your talents, your life experiences, your very attitude toward life. What makes you, you?

Ask yourself these questions:

What life experiences have prepared me for this position or industry?

What talents do I have outside the work place that could apply to this position?

What attitudes and traits do I have that could apply to this position or make this company better? (For example, optimism, problem solver, energetic.)

What education experience do I have, besides a degree, what specific courses did I take that apply to this position?

What are some specific work experience situations and accomplishments have I encountered that apply to this position?

What skills or talents do you have that won't necessarily fit on your resume? Such as attention to detail, great proofreader, etc.

Once you have a list of what makes you unique, you will be able to make yourself stand out among other candidates. While this information is not likely going to be on your resume, you can include it in your cover letter or in your interview answers and conversations.

When you bring up your special and unique personality traits, apply them to the position and the company. Let the interviewer know that you have these traits, and how they will benefit the position and the company. This will not only help you stand out among other candidates, it will also show the interviewer that you have put a lot of thought into what makes you the right fit for the job.

## Chapter 5: Initial Introductions

Initial introductions are enduring ones. Frequently they are made even before the meeting begins, throughout the requisition process. Moreover, first impressions are usually the lasting ones. Therefore, be sure to make an impact right away.

The first time you get a call from an organization regarding a job, you must realize that this is your first interaction, and it is just as important as the job interview. Voice messages may be the manager's initial introduction of you. Therefore, the message on your voice-mail or voice informing ought to be considerate and professional.

Also, inform everybody who may address the phone that business calls may take a swing at whenever. On the off chance that you feel your flat mates or parts of family unit are questionable, think about posting as a message or mobile phone number.

Make sure to deal with your mobile phone calls suitably.

Here are a few things that you must remember during your first introductions and interactions:

*Dress Appropriately*

Be certain, professional and pleasant when relating in individual, via mail, telephone or email.

Any time you cooperate with a potential business or anybody on their staff, envision that they are evaluating you.

The individual noting your inquiries or taking your provision may be the CEO sitting in for the receptionist on a break. You never know!

*Dress Professionally for the Position*

Being dressed somewhat more formally than your Interviewers is OK. It shows regard for them, the position, and the organization.

Get a lot of slumber the prior night. Your physical appearance will be busy best when you are alarm and rested.

Research industry desires in regards to clothing. This could be basically strolling, through the hall of the working environment, to watch how workers dress.

Avoid aromas and cologne

Arrange To Reach On Time

Know where to stop/how to enter a building.

Map your course to the meeting site.

Plan to arrive 10-15 minutes early.

Meet Graciously With The Secretary

The assistant is one of the first workers of the organization you will meet. While receptionists may not be settling on procuring choices, they will surely convey their impressions to the questioner.

Introduce yourself to the assistant and let them know the reason for the visit, and the questioner's name.

Thank the assistant for support.

Greet The Questioner Well

Greet your questioner utilizing Mr., Mrs. Or Ms.

Tell the questioner your name.

Shake their hand.

Wait to be offered a seat before sitting.

**Chapter 6: Top Job Interview Questions**

How does this position with our company factor into your ideal career plan?

Many people struggle to answer this question because it's just as difficult as "what's your five-year plan?" or "what are your goals in life?" Some people have their entire lives planned out, but if you're not one of them you might have no idea what you're going to be doing that far ahead. This is even trickier if you are just entering the workforce and you're still finding out which jobs you like and which ones you don't. However, employers really prefer somebody with a plan, not just somebody who's going with the flow.

Besides the obvious motivator of money, what inspires you to put time and effort into your work? What pushes you to challenge yourself, try new things, work harder, and achieve your goals? They want to know that you have a vision in your head and that you can make a plan. Your answer will give the interviewer insight into whether you really want this job or whether you really just need a job. That's really what they're asking - why do you want this job specifically?

With this in mind, a good place to start is with the skills and experience you hope to gain from the job. For example, "I hope that my career path will serve me and I will serve it. I want to grow professionally today so that I can contribute even more in my next role tomorrow, which will reward me when it comes to finances, my professional life, and my personal life. This position is a role that will help me grow, learn, and develop my skills, so professionally it is an excellent choice for me. As my skills improve, I will be rewarded with greater financial compensation as well as increased personal satisfaction. This position is a stepping stone for me, and it's a wonderful opportunity for me to grow and learn."

If you do have a goal in mind, discuss how the job will help you reach your goal. However, don't get too specific. Try something like "I will fulfill the needs of this position and make it valuable, I will grow my skills in order to help the company improve, and I eventually hope to take on roles that have a greater amount of responsibility." Answering using these guidelines will show your ambition without displaying any negative things, such as posing yourself as a threat to your interviewer's position. Basically, you don't need a rock-solid plan to give a satisfactory response. As long as you prove you're hoping to get more than just a paycheck out of the job, you should be all right.

Have you ever had issues with a coworker at any of your previous jobs? If so, how have you handled it?

This question is very specific, but they're really trying to gauge your reactions to difficult situations. Often, it is framed in different ways during behavioral interviews. The interviewer wants to know what your judgement is like and how well you make decisions. They want to know how you handle stressful situations, so you need to make sure your answer covers that. In this specific example, you have to discuss how you've handled a difficult colleague.

If this hasn't happened to you, you can say so. For example, "Luckily, I have never been placed in that situation. I have never had a coworker speak directly to me. Somebody has criticized me to my boss before, and due to her bigger role it was a difficult situation. However, she realized that the other person's criticism came from his jealousy and fear because I was a threat to his job. My boss then told me about the situation and we discussed ways for me to seem less threatening, so I just ended up avoiding getting in his way. I didn't confront him personally because that would have been unnecessary and unproductive."

Some people have been in situations where it was easiest to speak to the person themselves and discuss how the comments were harmful to them, their coworker, and the overall work environment. Some people bring the issue to their superior, but that's basically admitting that you can't handle it on your own. Some people go to Human Resources to file a complaint, but again, it's like saying you can't control it on your own.

If you've been lucky enough to not deal with any problem coworkers, just say that and don't guess as to how you might handle it. When interviewing with a company, you need to be thinking strategically, which does not include "what if" scenarios. If you've had to deal with problem coworkers, keep your answer upbeat and positive. Don't talk about going to HR, reporting them to your boss, or what a jerk the other person was. Don't talk about being happy to leave them behind at the other job. Basically, don't focus on the negative. Even if the situation wasn't your fault, complaining casts you in a negative light. You want your story to project your professional behavior, your ability to handle tricky situations without any help, and your habit of reaching positive outcomes.

How long do you think it will be before you are able to make an important contribution to our company?

This is a great question. It's the perfect chance for you to show off and tell them all about your 30-60-90 day plan. The plan itself is rather simple: it's the steps you plan to take during your first three months in a new job in order to learn the ropes and become a successful member of the team, or leader of the team if that is what the position entails. Generally, the first month of a new job involves training and becoming familiar with the company's systems and procedures. By the third month, you should be able to initiate things on your own, whether they be sales, projects, or policies. The more detail you give to the interviewer, the better.

Why are these 30-60-90 day plans so important? First off, the time and research required to make a good plan shows that you are knowledgeable and well-prepared, which is always an impressive thing for a company to see. It makes it obvious that you have an idea of what you'll be doing, even if the job itself is new to you. Second, these plans show hiring managers that you have the drive, enthusiasm, personal responsibility, initiative, and goal-setting traits that they are looking for. Third, as you walk the interviewer through your plan, they will begin to visualize you in the job as well. Once they start to see you in the position you're interviewing for, chances are higher they'll give you the job.

Sometimes these plans will get you a job offer right there, or get you a position better than the one you were interviewing for, or get you the job even though there is a more qualified candidate. If you're looking for the key to job interviews, this is it right here. Before your next interview, take the time to make a 30-60-90 day plan. This way, when the interviewer wants to know how long it will be before you can make an important contribution, you'll be ready.

"6 months maybe?" and "Sometimes it takes me a while to get settled but I want to see progress as well!" aren't sufficient. Your plan will give you a more solid foundation. It will let you say, "I have a plan for how to get myself on track as quickly as possible, do you mind giving me some feedback on it?" They'll accept, and you'll get a chance to tell them all the details and see what they think. Even if the plan isn't entirely correct, the conversation that follows will likely be one of your best interviews ever.

How long do you intend on keeping this job?

It sounds like they're asking about your future plans, but they're not. They don't want to know your career goals or your 5-year plan. It's a quick question that can be given an equally quick answer, and the one I like to use is "how long do you intend on keeping me?". Another option is "I'd like to work here for as long as possible because I'd like to avoid changing jobs. I'm willing to deal with the learning curves and everything else because I prefer to have a history with coworkers and feel like I'm able to rely on them." Lots of people can make this question work in their favor.

If your previous job was long-term, mention that. "I spent twelve years at my last job, do you think that kind of longevity is possible here too?" If none of your past jobs lasted very long, you want them to understand why that happened, but only if it makes you look good. Some scenarios have nothing to do with your performance in the job - for example, maybe there was a reduction in their employees or a round of layoffs and they followed the first-in-first-out policy, so you had to leave. If you enjoyed it there, say you would have preferred not to leave. Maybe you were working for a small company, your skills expanded beyond what they needed, and you had to leave in order to grow professionally.

That's something that everybody will understand, and both explanations include factors out of your control, which prevents any negative reflections on you. However, not everybody has a good excuse like this. In this case, an open confession might be best. For example, "I left too soon because I thought I had better prospects elsewhere, but now I know how to avoid that mistake." Admitting your mistake is all right as long as you talk about how you've learned from it since then. If the company chooses to hire you, they are making an investment. It takes both money and time to hire you, train you, and make sure you are settled in your new role and performing to your full potential. They don't want to put in that effort just to have you leave after a few months, so make sure to address that concern during your interview.

How much did you earn at your previous job? If you are still working, how much do you currently make?

This question is one of the most uncomfortable interview questions. It's a big one, and nobody wants to be the first to give a number. Don't let this question stress you out, there are actually some easy ways to handle it. If this salary question pops us before you've decided on an offer, try to deflect it and avoid it for as long as possible. Never bring it up yourself, and avoid money until you can get the interviewer to fall in love with you. Once they've decided that they like you and they want you in their company, you can use that as a bargaining chip to help negotiate a salary that is right for you.

If deflecting or avoiding the question is not possible, there are two options: be honest about how much money you make since it's not relevant in this position, or refuse to disclose how much money you make since it's not relevant in this position. Saying that the information is irrelevant works because generally the job you're trying to get is a step up from the last one. In that case, the money you made previously doesn't matter simply because the jobs are different. Personally, I don't think telling them your previous salary is a big issue. I have been a recruiter before, so I know from experience that companies have a salary range they are willing to pay for each position, and no recruiter makes an offer beyond that.

The goal of this question is for them to determine whether or not they can afford to hire you. This is another point where taking the time to do some research can be helpful. If you have an idea of what people in that position are generally paid in that area of the country, you will know whether or not their offer is a good one. If they try to get you to work for cheap, you'll notice and be able to negotiate with your own offer.

Many people don't feel comfortable talking about their salary. In this case, you can say something along the lines of, "My previous job is too different from this one for me to be comfortable discussing my salary. I'd prefer to answer questions about my qualifications and skills so that we can see whether or not I'm the right person for this job. If that discussion works out, I'm sure we can find common ground on my salary as well. I'm excited for the opportunity to work here." Another option is to hand the question back to them: "What does the salary range you offer for this job look like?" Once they answer, state that you are happy with that range and that if you were offered something within it, you would not turn down the job due to concerns about money.

Always remember that each interview is different. A negotiation cannot be figured out with a formula. You've got to stay light on your feet, assess the situation, and see how far you can get. One thing is for sure, though - the more time you take to research and prepare beforehand, the better off you'll be.

Was your work relationship with your past supervisor a good one?

This question is the hiring manager asking about your attitude. They don't really care about your boss, they care about your attitude towards your boss. Your past behavior is a good indicator of your future performance, and the company is well aware of this. They want to know whether you're the type to throw your boss under the bus. Are you going to complain about misunderstandings, or are you going to talk about what you've learned? This question is very common in job interviews, so be prepared.

If you're lucky, you and your boss had a great relationship. Even in this case, make sure to talk about what you learned from them and your relationship, especially when it comes to skills that will help you at the company. They don't just want to hear that it was good, they want to know that you learned something. They want people who are coachable and able to use criticism to improve.

If your relationship wasn't great, try to put a positive spin on your answer, but don't lie outright. Never, ever lie outright - first, it's dishonest. Second, there are very few people in the world who don't give off subtle signals when they lie, and the hiring manager will pick up on them. Instead, think of the lessons you gained from that relationship. Even in negative relationships, chances are you've learned something. Any negativity you show will only hurt yourself, not your former boss. You'll look whiny. However, it is possible to turn an unhappy relationship into a new opportunity. For example, if you and your boss has vastly different personalities, you can say so. For example: "We had two very different personalities that didn't always mesh well, but I learned ways to adapt to somebody else's work style and overall it made me into a pretty well-rounded employee."

If you've had a horrible boss it may take some time to find the positives, but it's well worth the time. Your ability to stay upbeat and find the bright side even when dealing with stress will reflect very well on you. Just keep your goal in mind: you want this job. You really need to sell yourself, so always bring the conversation back to what you've learned from previous bosses that will help you be successful with this one. If you have a situation that you can't possibly spin in a positive light, try meeting with a career coach.

## Chapter 7: The Big Question: What Qualities Are Interviewers Looking For?

At the very core of every clueless applicant is the wish that they knew what exactly interviewers are looking for. Things would be easier if there was a golden set of rules to follow all the time.

Unfortunately, this is not the case. This is because different companies have different standards and different requirements for a particular position. Some companies will really value punctuality and will reject you if you arrive late. Others will really scrutinize your work history and ask you all sorts of questions about your background.

Despite that, there are a few common qualities that will always improve your chances when you attend an interview.

Professionalism

You're not just meeting one person in one cubicle. You're meeting a whole company and your prospective employer. By that virtue alone, they deserve a certain degree of respect and courtesy.

Part of that means being on time or early. If it is possible, plan your commute/drive ahead of time and intend to arrive at least 15 minutes earlier than your schedule. This will give you some time to freshen up and get settled in so that you're not rattled when they call your name.

Another part of professionalism is a bit of formal language. Unless instructed otherwise, it's best you call your interviewer sir or ma'am to be on the safe side. This will show that you came to talk about business and you're serious. Don't worry if your interviewer asks you to call them by their first name, it's an indication that they want you to feel comfortable.

Professionalism isn't just shown in those cases. It also comes out in your answers. Regardless of your experiences with your previous employers, it's taboo to bad-mouth them when the topic shifts to your work history. Remember; if you can bad-mouth your ex-boss, what's to stop them from thinking you won't do it to them as well?

Communication Skills

No matter what kind of job you're aiming for, communication skills will always add value to your scorecard. If you can talk the talk, then there's a good chance you can walk the walk with ease.

You don't necessarily have to over-exert yourself here; but you want to make sure you can deliver. Will you be able to get your ideas across to the interviewer? Do you answer in complete sentences or with short and boring Yes and No answers?

Are you still struggling with your prepositions? Mixing up on, in and at? What about longer explanations? Are you able to relay a full story from start to finish without stuttering and struggling for words? Do you stall for time when asked to talk about past experiences because you're not too good with verb tenses?

Being able to express yourself with ease is the goal here. If your interviewer finds you easy to understand, it's easier for them to give you the job.

This means brushing up on your grammar if you have to. Go back to the books and try some mock-interviews with a friend. Use the questions in the latter part of this manual and try to come up with some answers on the spot. That should serve as good practice exercises for the big day.

Flexibility

It goes without saying that every job will have its ups and downs. The business world is no stranger to change; so you shouldn't be either.

This is where being flexible shines the most. Can you handle difficult and most often impromptu situations? Have you ever had to take on a lot of responsibility with very little time to adjust and think? Are you capable of keeping up with changing business trends or company policies?

Have you ever had to render overtime because one of your colleagues was out sick? How about working on a weekend to finish a report that was supposed to have been done by someone else? Your interviewer wants to see if they can depend on you when the going gets tough.

Try to remember a time wherein you had to do one of these things. That experience will come in handy especially when your interviewer starts talking about your work experience. Couple that with some good communication skills and you have yourself a job offer.

The Technical Skills

Depending on the nature of the job you're hunting, you will also need to exhibit certain technical skills to show them that you can do the job well. This could mean anything in between operating heavy machinery to programming software for computers.

Although it's impossible to map every single technical skill available, there are a few skills that every beginner needs to have.

First is basic computer knowledge; and this doesn't mean browsing the internet. This covers both hardware and software. Can you do a hard reset on your desktop? Are you familiar with some basic troubleshooting steps? Can you locate all the USB ports on a computer? Are you capable of differentiating a router from a modem?

The next thing you would want is basic knowledge on common computer applications such as Microsoft Word and Microsoft Excel. Can you print the same document in both portrait and landscape? Are you familiar with making a spreadsheet complete with formulas? Can you adjust the indentation of the document you're typing?

If you're able to access this manual, there's a good chance you already have these basic skills. Despite that, it's always a good idea to see if you can still find your way around a computer before going to your interview.

The trouble with these qualities is showing your interviewer that you have them. Some companies will put you through tests to see you exhibit these skills, but what if they don't?

If your interviewer asks you if you can cover a certain technical skill, don't just say yes. Talk about the skill and do not forget to use any jargon involved with the skill. Explain your methods and techniques. This will exhibit competence and confidence at the same time.

Problem Solving

Your interviewer also needs to know if you're capable of taking care of problems when they arise under your watch. Are you capable of looking at a situation from different angles in order to find a solution? Do you always rely on instructions from management when something goes wrong or do you find a way to fix things to nip them in the bud before they get worse?

Unless your interviewer gives you a problem to solve, it would be difficult to exhibit this quality. Try talking about a time wherein you used a clever solution in a sticky situation to highlight this skill when you have the chance. This usually happens when the interviewer starts asking you questions like "tell me a time when…"

There is a section in this book dedicated to those kinds of questions. Be sure to go over it before actually going to your interview. The method indicated there is designed to be a clear and concise approach to highlighting your qualities.

## **Chapter 8**: **Useful Ways You Can Impress Your Interviewer**

An interview is the most common thing every job seeker would go through a lot many times in his career. It is an interaction of both the interviewer and interviewee to understand each other properly, discuss any questions, facts, or statements.

While it a two-way communication, most of the interviewees are hesitant to start a conversation with their interviewers because of the fear of being rejected. They think that asking questions from the employer may annoy him and create a biased and displeased feeling in his mind. Not every interview is easy, and every individual is not confident about himself and the interview. There may have been some interviews in which you didn't perform well, you're nervous, or didn't like the work environment or pay. There may be some interviews in which you gave your best but were not selected by the interviewer, and you kept thinking all night about what wrong did you do in your interview.

Having the necessary qualifications and skills may not always give you a 100 percent guarantee of being selected. Besides being excellent in academics, there are some other interviewer skills which are necessary to possess to impress your interviewer and get selected. You must possess the right attitude, personality, knowledge, and body language besides your academic qualification. Sometimes it is one of these factors only that companies reject individuals.

Sometimes, depending upon the type of job, a company may require a person who is extrovert or introvert, frank or serious, fluent, or full of skills. There are some other factors, too, that may result in your rejection. Sometimes it may be your dressing sense or inability to carry all the necessary documents. Getting rejected in

3 or 4 interviews is an excellent thing that you don't have to worry about. Start again and carry yourself positively. But if we are being rejected, again and again, it is a matter of concern. You have to look deep and find out the factors which you have to work upon for your success Look upon all the factors – external (dressing sense), internal (attitude, tone of voice, commitment), social (conversation skills) and personality-related (extrovert, introvert, frank, serious).

Interviewer Pre-Preparation

If you are serious enough for a job or a company, then you may have to prepare beforehand for a lot of things to combat any factors responsible for your failure.

If not interested in a company or post: Even if you don't find a job opportunity interesting, go for the interview anyway. This helps in building up future contacts of job opportunities. Moreover, you learn about the company, their work environment, and the interview conducted builds up the confidence in you for future interviews.

Prepare a file with all necessary documents: Carry all the required documents in a well-organized file. Reorganize your CV according to the job profile and work upon choosing the appropriate references too. Carry 2-3 extra copies of your CV and remember not to forget any documents related to what you have mentioned in your CV. Always prepare your file according to the job profile. Carry the latest and eligible documents only. The interviewer doesn't want to see the certificates of activities performed on your 10th.

Prepare a short story of your skills: If you are not that good in describing yourself and your abilities, prepare a short story about it. Stories are easy to remember both for you and the interviewer. Rehearse the storyline and get it made concrete so that any chances of inability to speak yourself are minimized.

Pre-search for the location and distance: Be on time. If in the first meeting itself you reach late, it would not yield a good impression of your punctuality. Search for the location, nearest points, and ideal mode of transport by researching Google maps. Reach the destination 30 minutes early. However, avoid reaching too soon as it may pressurize the interview conducting team.

Do thorough research: Do thorough research about the company, its mission statement, history, awards & achievements, and product offerings. This is important as the interviewer often asks their candidates questions related to their company. They want to check whether the candidate is serious enough about the job and company or not. Hence, it is recommended to research about all the necessary information beforehand.

Read up the current affairs: Have a thorough knowledge of current affairs and current news related to your job. For example, if you are going for a financial analyst job, you should have a full understanding of current economic and financial conditions and new laws being worked upon.

Re-organize your social media: Nowadays, there are many profiles for which the information of the social media channels you use are equally important for the interviewer. So delete any quotes, pictures, status, or discussions that may sound profane or objecting to your recruiter.

On the interview day morning

Dress formally and avoid flashy ornaments: Truly said-"The first impression is the last impression." Dress up in proper formals. Your hair should be neatly combed, and nails should be trimmed properly. Never wear something too fancy for an interview. Accessories such as belt and small earrings are desirable but avoid any accessory, which is too fancy or flashy. Avoid any strong perfumes and fragrances, which may distract the interviewers. Avoid heavy makeup and strong shades of lipstick. These are some small crumbs which, when not worked upon properly, can decrease your selection probability.

Go for a short break: After reaching your interview destination, make sure to go to the restroom and check your hair, face, teeth, and clothes. Give the last touch up to your hair, check for any dirt on the shoes, wash your hands to remove any sweat or dust.

Waiting room etiquettes: In the waiting room, be kind to everyone. Be polite and avoid showing your hurry and nervousness. Avoid using phones as they are most likely to convey some bad news, which may distress you and distract your focus.

During your interview

See for your body language: Your body language speaks a lot about you. The interviewer can know what type of personality you have by noticing your hand movements, eye movements, and talking fluency. Never wear lanky clothes or uncomfortable footwear, which makes it awkward for you to walk in for the interview.

Greeting your interviewer: Greet your interviewer with a smile and a firm handshake. Remember, your hands should not be shaking or full of sweat. Don't sit like a wax statue in a tight position. While talking, use your hands to explain things. Make an eye to eye contact with the interviewer. Avoid laughing and being too frank while talking. Don't move your arms and legs here and there. Avoid touching your face, rubbing your nose, manage hair strands. A proper posture and body movements should be worked upon thoroughly and should be maintained not only inside the interview room but also in the waiting hall.

Have an ideal tone of voice: Whatever be your voice tone, you have to adjust it according to the conditions. In an interview, it is necessary to convey a polite and gentle tone. Your voice should express your interest, courteousness, and commitment towards the job and company. Avoid opting for a voice that is too hard to hear as well as a tone too harsh to hear and which may also convey your arrogance and attitude. Don't speak in a hurry, talk about everything clearly, and give stress on essential words.

Ask your interviewer a few questions: It is advised to ask your interviewer a few questions. It may be about the company, the work, challenges, etc. Ask what does the company values the most, what you may be learning out of your job, what is the company's future goals. If you don't ask questions and leave without a conversation from your side, it implies either you didn't understand the work, or you are uninterested in the company.

Describe yourself and your talents: Give a fledged description about what interview skills you developed from your last experience at different companies. Showcase all your abilities and skills with full confidence and energy. If, however, at any company, your experience was not good, never say bad things about your former employers. It builds up a negative image of you, and some employers may dislike this attitude of yours. Avoid talking about the salary in the first meeting. These questions can be discussed in the later stages of selection.

Be sure for what you write: Never write any skill, talent which you cannot perform with full confidence. If your interviewer tells you to show one of those skills, and you don't do it correctly and confidently, it may decrease your points, and you may also feel embarrassed.

Convince your interviewer: Display yourself in such a manner that your interviewer is highly impressed with your personality, thoughts, and skills. Give examples of how you can prove to be an asset for the company, what you are having which others are lacking, and showcase your commitment towards the organization. Always tell the truth. Never boast your skills and talents, which may convey your egotism.

Gather up with ease: At the end of the interview, gather your files and documents calmly and with a smile. Gathering things quickly may lead to dropping things or documents, which may make you embarrassed. Have a handshake with your interviewer and say thank you. Walk towards the door slowly and with confidence.

Send a follow-up mail: After your interview session, it is advised to send a thank you note to the employer through email. This might not seem fruitful to you, but these tiny doings can yield a good reputation and liking of the employer towards you. You can build a reputation that people would look up to, and you would be considered to be amongst the best relationship builder.

The interview is a responsible and serious task both for the interviewer and the interviewee. The Interviewer also has a lot of pressure regarding who to choose, not to become partial or unfair with any interviewee, to select the right employee who proves to be an asset for the company and who becomes a permanent employee with his full commitment.

In the same way, an interview is nervous about impressing the interviewer, showing all the positive qualities and skills, and hiding any negative ones, which may reduce his chances of selection.

Sometimes this pressure creates a hindrance and makes it furthermore challenging to go for an interview. If you get too nervous about the interview, you may need some personality development classes. Be positive whatever the result be. With every interview conducted, you will learn about what you are good in, what you have to work upon, what impressed your interviewer, and what etiquette you have to work upon further. Never think anything wrong about your interviewer. Place yourself in his shoes and feel the pressure of selecting the right employee. Recognize your weaknesses and work thoroughly upon them.

Also, note that you don't have to pretend what you aren't. Never act yourself too much, which may shock the recruiter afterward. Though working on body language and personality is essential but showcase only those qualities which you can carry conveniently after the selection process too.

Developing a responsible and committed attitude towards your job and company is essential, and this feeling should come from inside and not only during the interview day. Always work with your full potential at every job. This will make up the right image of you in the eyes of the employer so that in future, if you have to give his references, you feel confident to do that. Develop positive interpersonal relationships in every work environment, which will not only create the right image of you but also improve your personal conversational and social skills.

**Chapter 9: Your Fears**

Predict the best outcome possible.

The Fear Response

WHEN A THREATENING EVENT OCCURS, the effects of fear are felt in the body, even when the physical body isn't threatened.

The emotional brain which is the headquarters for survival instincts that are activated in the fear response, evolved when you were an infant, long before you were able to think things through.

That's why the feeling state of anxiety is so deeply rooted, and is resistant to thoughts. At every stage of life, a threat to your physical or emotional safety will trigger the fear response in a flash.

The fear that is familiar to all of us is a survival mechanism that is activated with urgency by any perceived danger, in the part of the brain called the amygdala – a set of neurons that are responsible for processing our emotions.

When you perceive danger and become fearful, or when you experience a threat to your mental, emotional, or physical self, your amygdala signals the adrenal glands to begin to release into your blood stream the stress hormones, adrenaline and noradrenaline. This activates the automatic stress response of fight, flight, or freeze, to prepare you to fight or flee the danger.

At this point, your heart rate speeds up and your blood pressure rises. Blood pounds in your head, while your breathing becomes rapid and shallow, and your eyes dart. These primitive reactions are meant to prepare you to encounter an assailant. Blood that rushes to your extremities allows you to stand and fight the perceived danger, or run from it. Accordingly, your hands tighten and forearms become heavy, and you become hyper-alert, anxious, and ready to defend, despite the fact that an assailant is not ever likely to appear!

All of these primitive reactions are automatic, generated from the emotional aspect of your brain. They don't require any conscious decisions on your part.

In primitive times, you might have faced a saber-tooth tiger and perhaps clubbed it over the head, or maybe you ran from it as fast as you could. In either case, if you caught sight of a second tiger stalking you, it's likely you would have frozen in fear right there on the spot.

Today, it's uncommon to have to defend ourselves physically. More probable at this point in time, most perceived threats will be to our thoughts and feelings.

No matter the threat, the stress responses of fight, flight, and freeze are hard-wired into our brains.

Earlier, when you used your imagination to explore the balance beam, your brain believed the experience, because it's unable to distinguish between a real event and an imagined one.

A threat is a threat, despite whether the danger is mental, emotional, physical, or imagined. The stress responses that we feel are in reaction to our fear of a perceived attack, whether or not actual danger exists. Regardless, the same primitive responses occur.

Your stress response is activated and you prepare to fight or flee.

Sometimes, as with the second tiger stalking you, the terror is so great you cannot move.

When you're terrified, your cognition – the thinking part of you – freezes.

That's why it's difficult to form a coherent sentence when you're angry, or why you struggle to remember a fact or detail when you're rattled.

Later, when the threat passes, your fear subsides, and you get your brain back.

The Anxiety Response

If you feel anxious, you're not alone.

Anxiety, which is closely connected to fear, is another automatic stress response during which your amygdala, when triggered by external events, sends signals to the adrenal glands to release stress hormones into your blood stream.

Uncertainty about the future is a reality for many of us, and uncertainty and worry can quickly set the anxiety response into motion.

Although some people may seem invincible, anxiety can be provoked in any of us.

When we're anxious, our brain is focused on the future, and predicts that something bad is about to happen. This puts us out of balance.

At any life stage, and especially during stressful times such as a job search, anxiety can strike when our thoughts about accepting that we don't know what the future holds, and wondering what lies ahead of us tip out of balance. Our thoughts might begin to morph into worrying about the future.

When we're out of balance we talk too much, tell too much, ask too much, control too much – and sometimes do the opposite of any of those actions.

Even when we're just a little bit nervous, our sense organs are on high alert. When that happens, we easily fall back on our automatic behavior, and retreat into a comfort zone where our choices are limited to a restricted range of options.

As an example, for some of us, the fear of punishment in childhood resulted in hyper-obedient adolescents and adults who, despite being grown, are terrified of judgment.

Paradoxically, if at some point we become anxious and retreat to the emotional safety of a comfort zone, our anxious response may be perceived by others as an indication that we're oppositional.

Sadly, anxious youth are too often labelled difficult and oppositional, when their behavior is anything but.

The stress responses of anxiety tend to be flight and freeze.

Once the anxiety response is set in motion, the effects can be long-term and enduring.

As with the fear response, the activation of anxiety causes the brain to repeatedly signal the release of stress hormones until the mind eventually quiets, as a result of whatever conscious or unconscious methods are used to soothe the distress.

Whether you experience fear or anxiety, your brain registers that you're in danger.

Fear is a quick dash, while anxiety can feel more like a long-distance foot race, that's run barefoot over jagged glass.

It bears repeating: it doesn't matter if the danger is real or if it's imagined.

You may feel uncomfortable in conflict situations. If your automatic stress response is to flee disagreements, you'll leave. In the extreme, maybe you won't show up at all.

If you're afraid of appearing foolish, you could be terrified to share your ideas and thoughts. You might choke up when you disagree with someone, or become tearful in the face of criticism.

When your thoughts are overwhelmed by the stress of the situation, you're likely to freeze; be unable to gather your thoughts or speak in an organized manner.

Just as in the fear response, when we feel anxious and stressed, our cognition shuts down.

You might remember being called on in school to give an answer you were unsure of, and with the pressure to give a response, your brain suddenly was blank. That's what happens when your cognition shuts down. When we're anxious, thinking, remembering, and sorting simple details becomes a colossal struggle.

Fear and anxiety are brain events, triggered by our thoughts.

Mindfulness restores cognition and overrides anxious thoughts by placing our awareness in the present moment – which is the only point at which we are free from worry.

The mindfulness process doesn't happen by chance.

It's intentional, and requires some effort and directed attention.

Fear, Anxiety and the Brain: A Mindful Approach

Over time, fear and anxiety, activated by thoughts that are often below the level of consciousness can become an automatic defense against attempting new behaviours, participating in new experiences, and venturing into a new physical or psychological territory.

Moving forward and unwinding our automatic responses requires us to bring mindfulness into the process, with the awareness that long-standing anxious thought patterns can readily slip forward and take control of our thinking.

Anxious thoughts can be a useful nudge to remind you to focus on your breathing, and take steps to return your thoughts into balance.

Calming our anxiety through the mindful state of relaxed attention in the present moment, is said to place us in a tranquil condition that is known as flow.

Flow is a mode of hyper-awareness that's often intentionally accessed by athletes, musicians, artists, and other individuals who are aware of the power it yields to achieve an exceptional outcome and transform their experience.

When we're in flow, we're said to be in the zone, a psychological state that can influence our intellect, creativity, and physical performance, during which we're alert and focused in the moment.

Two examples of flow come to mind from my own experience. In the first, while in a tennis seminar, the instructor invited me to demonstrate a volleying technique we were just learning. I felt extreme anxiety to be demonstrating the technique to the other participants, which pushed me into a state of hyper-focus, and into the present. The intensity of the experience engulfed me. As I volleyed with the tennis pro, my mind perceived an expansion of time. All my senses were alerted.

Soon I had an awareness that my attention was centered inside the tennis ball, and that my physical self was somehow connected to the ball. My muscles reacted with astounding precision.

My tennis ability in those minutes in flow far exceeded any actual skill I possessed either before or at any time after the event. Remarkably, many years later, my muscle memory of that occurrence remains clear.

In flow, time appears to speed up or slow down.

This phenomenon was even more amplified in a second example, when a vehicle in which I was a front-seat passenger was broadsided in an intersection. Moments before impact it felt as if time slowed to a crawl, and I became a witness to what was occurring. In an implausibly trance-like state I observed the passenger window beside me shatter, slow-motion, into thousands of pebbles that sprayed the vehicle's interior. It was only later, after I was pulled from the vehicle, that my perception of time returned to normal.

In both of my personal examples, and in other instances where being in the zone and experiencing flow have occurred in my life, the predominant feature has been concentrated and riveted attention that took charge of my anxiety while the event was taking place.

You may remember times in your own life when the stakes were extremely high and you observed the phenomenon of flow having an impact.

Perhaps, like many people, you remember a situation of lesser consequence, when a fragile object was knocked from a counter, slipped through your hands, and was falling towards the floor.

Through some extraordinary feat of athleticism and coordination, astonishingly you caught the object mid-flight! Some aspect of your consciousness in those moments took charge of the event, focused your attention, and directed the outcome before your eyes.

I use these examples of flow to illustrate the extraordinary power of mindful attention.

Your thoughts create your reality.

Gaining mastery over our thoughts is a life-long pursuit. Despite our best efforts, we can become embarrassed about a remark we've made, or some action we've taken, feel anxious about an event, or suffer disappointment over some aspect of our self.

Sometimes it's difficult to remain in the moment, separate our process from the outcome, and keep up our spirits.


You are not your results!

During moments of panic or dread, all of us know what it's like to be socially awkward, complete with clammy palms and flop-sweat. Sometimes we fuss over unnecessary details, and can be obsessed with gadgets. We've all had bad hair days and made clothing choices that are just wrong. We can be hyper-focused, tedious, and painfully dull.

At times we've all cracked up at our own lame jokes, have been blind to social cues, given long-winded explanations, and been entirely unaware that no one is even slightly interested in what we're talking about. Without question, all of us are nerdy.

Believe it. Everyone has nerdy parts. No matter how awesome and amazing another person appears, each and every day, they and everyone else fight a private battle with their own particular insecurities.

When you embrace the nerd that you are, your act of self-acceptance raises your consciousness.

With self-acceptance, your self-esteem becomes shatter-proof, at least for the time being, and let's face it, the present moment is all there is.

It's hard to take yourself seriously while affirming the brilliance of your nerd-dom.

On the following page you'll find the Nerd Declaration, a tool that will release you from self-judgment, cultivate your sense of humour, and assist you to lighten up.

The declaration of your nerd-dom is the ultimate strength contract and affirmation. Learn it!

Say it often:

I am a nerd.

I always was a nerd.

I always will be a nerd.

There is no hope.

wtf! I'm going for it anyway!

## Chapter 10: Maintaining Rapport And Respect

Prior conversations can be of help, but in the context of an interview, it is most likely that you will be talking with someone you have just met for a period of twenty minutes or so. According to experts, you need to maximize the meanings that are transmitted by both your words and the actions that go with them.

Rapport is created with the help of the subconscious. It is primarily assisted by non-verbal signs. Among the signals that usually figure in the list are the following: positioning of the body parts, the movement and rhythm of the body, the level of eye contact, the kind of facial expression, and the tone of the voice.

The best illustration here is when you are talking with a close friend. After a minute or two, if you will look closely and pay attention to your non-verbal cues, the tendency is for each of you to copy each other's gestures, movements, and facial expressions, among others. Rapport is usually created in a natural and instinctive manner. It acts as our line of defense against possible conflicts. Throughout the history of mankind, it is quite clear that rapport is effective in maintaining day-to-day peace and harmony.

During an interview, it is important to build rapport with the interviewer. To do this, you need to appropriately use your body language. Be aware of the signs that you are sending and be conscious of the signals being sent by your interviewer. The non-verbal communication should be parallel to the verbal communication. That way, you will appear more pleasant, prepared, open, and relaxed.

When your interviewer is saying something, try to reflect back and clarify whenever there arises any difficulty. This will help you in showing that you are listening closely. Additionally, you will appear more empathic and sensitive.

Also, you have to be careful in using your voice. Project it properly. Deliver what you wish to say in such a way that it reflects your genuine interest. Also, try to stabilize your tone and hide the tense of nervous feeling. It is best to take your time when speaking. Talking quickly will only make you appear stressed or nervous or tense. Furthermore, you can always adjust your pitch, tone, pace, and volume to suit your intention.

There are other behaviors that prove to be helpful in building rapport. Here are some of the following:

When seated and you wish to project that you are truly interested in what the interviewer is saying, try leaning forward a bit. The hands should be open and the legs and the arms of the person should not be crossed. This kind of non-verbal cue will not only send the message that you are truly listening. This will also help you feel a bit more relaxed.

Establish eye contact, but do not overdo it. The optimal value would be look at the one you are speaking with around sixty percent of the time. Overdoing this will make your interviewer feel uncomfortable. Meanwhile, doing it less than 60 percent of the time might make your interviewer feel that you are not listening or that you are not paying attention.

Maintain that sweet smile throughout the interview.

Remember your interviewer's name. Addressing him using his name will make him feel a bit more important. It is a recognition that you are capable of being respectful.

When asking questions, choose open-ended ones. Open-ended questions are questions that require well-thought of answers or responses. They are not your typical "yes or no" questions.

Offer feedbacks to show that you can summarize or reflect on what the interviewer is saying. Aside from building rapport, this will help in clarifying any misunderstandings even before they get bigger.

Use previous statements given by the interviewer in your answers to show that you are truly listening.

Even if you are just a mere interviewee, try to show empathy. This can be demonstrated by expressing your understanding of how your interviewee feels on certain issues or matters.

When you do not know the answer, say it directly. Never pretend that you know the answer or do not try to lie just to come up with an answer. Admitting mistakes is one of the most interesting and most admirable things that an applicant can do.

These will work well if you will try to be more genuine. You may also offer a compliment if it is well-deserved. Finally, maintain your politeness.

## Chapter 11: Things You Should Avoid In A Job Interview

In as much as you need to focus on the must-do things for a job interview, it is also essential that you know the things you shouldn't do.

1. Too casual at greeting

As a result of over excitement, many candidates end up making this mistake. Avoid greeting without proper eye contact as it is considered impolite and unprofessional. These little mistakes made by candidates are often noted by the interviewer, so ensure to put up good manners when going for an interview.

2. Questionable documents

This is another mistake you should avoid making. Ensure to check your documents accurately and make sure they are complete before going for an interview, as incomplete records could make you lose your chances of getting the job. The missing information when asked about by your interviewer could embarrass you.

3. Arriving late

As stated earlier, ensure to arrive at least 10-15 minutes more prior than the scheduled time for the interview. As coming late might keep the interviewers waiting, and this may create doubt about hiring you as they are not sure if you have proper time management skill.

4. Absence

If anything comes up that might likely lead to absence, like illness, car trouble, delays caused by traffic, etc. ensure to inform your contact person and apologize for your lateness or absence. Make sure to state the reason behind this development as this would enable the interviewer to comprehend your situation.

5. A lack of interest in the employer

A lack of interest in knowing the employer of the company is a mistake that many candidates make. Do some research to get proper information about who your employer is because if you are hired, you are automatically working for that person. So do proper research and gather information about the employer before the interview.

6. Improper appearance

Appearance gives the first impression about you to your interviewer. Wear professional clothes and avoid wearing worn out, dirty or rumpled clothes to your interview.

7. Improper clothing

Clothing is an essential thing in making an excellent first impression. Do not wear tight, short, or sexually provocative clothing to your interview. Make sure your clothes are clean, professional, and well ironed. Remember your interview venue is not for fashion.

8. Bad manners

Another thing to avoid during the interview is terrible manners such as stammering, playing with any object in your hand or straddling chairs, etc. Most of these actions are as a result of bad habits or nervousness, so relax and try to be as comfortable as possible.

9. Abrasive posture

Irritating attitudes like chewing gum, looking bored, yawning, sighing, keeping an eye on the clock, etc. are not what you should do in an interview.

10. Intellectual absence

Avoid being absent-minded in an interview as this poses as disrespectful to the interviewer. Listen to the questions attentively and answer them politely and correctly.

11. Being quick

This mistake is usually familiar with the first-time candidate and also experienced candidates too, who may think that they are keeping to time not knowing that they are creating a wrong impression. They tend to chatter, answering the questions as fast as they can. But in the mind of the interviewer, you are in a hurry to leave.

## 12. Over-estimation of your abilities

Avoid over-estimating your skills, don't think that you are the only one with all the capabilities. It's good to be confident about your abilities, but overconfidence and exaggeration may lead to losing the opportunity.

## 13. Don't talk about your personal life

One important thing in an interview is your ability to keep your personal and professional life separate. When answering any interview question related to your job or the company avoids digressing to your own life as this doesn't sit well with the interviewer.

## 14. Meaningless chit-chat

You must understand that applying the right words in places like an interview is very important. Unnecessary small talks are inappropriate and unprofessional. It gives the impression that you can't concentrate on essential things. Your words must be well considered and professional at all times in an interview.

15. Don't fidget or play

This is a common mistake made by interview candidates. Do not move around nervously or idly in an interview as this creates a wrong impression and an unprofessional look. If you have a habit of doing that, ensure to prepare properly before going for the interview.

## Chapter 12: Preparation

For the day of the interview, it is recommended to show up around 10 minutes early instead of just showing up on time. You want to set the tone and set the impression that you are reliable and that you can be on time. If you're not exactly sure where the job interview takes place, then it is a good idea to go to that part of town a couple of days before the interview and to see where exactly do you have to go. This way you will know exactly where to go and how much time it will take you to get there. Trust me, there's nothing worse than not getting to the job interview on time because you don't know where to go and it makes you feel like a buffoon. You will also be a lot calmer and confident if you have a plan and if you know exactly what you're doing. You always want to have some room for error and you should be especially careful if the interview is conducted during the hours when the traffic is bad.

It is necessary to do the research the company and the role you're applying for so that you have an understanding of what you will be taking part in and in which way you can add value. To go a step further, it is recommended to use resources other than only the company website such as news or social media. After you have gone through this data, then you can see how your skills and knowledge and what you have put on your resume correspond to and fit in there. If you are given information on the person or persons who will be interviewing you, then it is a good idea to see if that person has a presence on Linkedin so that you could see who you are dealing with and be even more prepared. Just remember that people on Linkedin can see when someone views their profile, so you may want to be careful with this.

Getting enough sleep is generally recommended for every night, but it is especially important to get this right on the night before the interview in order to do your best during the interview. Don't eat anything in the evening that may compromise sleep and make sure that in your bedroom it is so dark that you can't see anything other than the blackness. The temperature in the room should be a bit on the cooler side. It is also not recommended to do anything stimulating an hour or so before bed or to be around many electronic lights. Electronic lights emit so-called blue light which is a wavelength which, when absorbed by the eyes, stops melatonin from being released, melatonin being the hormone which makes people sleepy during the times of the day when they usually go to bed. To combat this you can also have an application such as flux installed on your devices which will block most of that blue light. It is also a good idea to purchase blue light blocking glasses and to wear the hour or two before going to bed.

It is necessary to be dressed for the occasion and to have clothes and other documentation laid out and ready before the day of the interview so that you don't have to waste time and nerves. Things like your CV, certifications, list of questions you want to ask and all the rest should be prepared and all in one place. It's even good to be aware of what the weather will be like so that you know if you will have to make some necessary adjustments in order to reach the interview. You should be aware of the appropriate dress code and to not be below that. There is no need to overcomplicate this, the most important factor is that the clothes fit you well.

One thing to remember is that the interview starts as soon as you enter the building and you should try to leave a good impression on everyone. For example, the person on the reception may be under instructions to observe everyone who shows up for the interview, so anyone who treats the receptionist haphazardly will have their points taken away. How you do one thing is how you do everything. Also, when you're sitting or standing in the waiting room, that is the worst time to be checking your phone since you never know who is watching. Just be there and wait, there will be plenty of time for checking the phone later during the day.

When the interview starts, just have a relaxed and open body language. Don't be afraid to take a little bit of space since you will look more confident and adopting such a power pose does actually influence your mood and your confidence. Instead of just answering a question point blank, it is recommended to try to steer the interview into an actual conversation by telling a story which will most likely put everyone at ease. The interview should begin and conclude with a proper handshake while maintaining eye contact. Also, thank people for their time and for the opportunity for the interview. A lot of people don't even get that opportunity.

## Chapter 13: Pass With Flying Colors

As you interview for jobs, you'll have an advantage toward getting the job of your dreams if you have an understanding of what interviewers want to hear. Along the same lines, you'll benefit from knowing some things you should never say in an interview. And then, you'll also want to convey to the interviewer that you have the soft skills which will ensure your standing as a valuable employee and place you above the other candidates for the same job. (For those of you who aren't familiar with soft skills, I'll explain that in more detail later in this chapter.)

11 Things Your Prospective Employer Wants to Hear.

When you interview for a job, you'll likely be asked a lot of questions. Some job candidates make the mistake of not understanding why the interviewer is asking the questions they're asking. If you have a feel for why your interviewer is asking the questions they're asking, you'll find it much easier to determine the things they want to hear from you. Here are some things that interviewers love to hear from candidates, in no particular order.

1) "I'm self-motivated. If you give me a project, I can take it from start to finish...and I can get it done in time. You won't have to micromanage me. I can work with minimal supervision."

2) "I take direction well. You won't have to tell me the same thing multiple times. If you tell me what to do once, you won't have to tell me again."

3) "I am a good communicator. I'll keep you and my co-workers updated on any projects I'm working on."

4) "I work and play well with others. I'm a team player, not a lone wolf."

5) "I can lead or I can follow. I do both well."

6) "I'm teachable. I'm quick to admit that I don't know everything and I'm willing and anxious to learn from others."

7) "I have the skills to do the job." (Reiterate your skills here.)

8) "I'm a good fit for this job and I'm a good fit for this company." (Detail why you're a good fit here.)

9) "I'm loyal. I'll be loyal to my supervisor and loyal to the company."

10) "My goals and objectives coincide with the mission and purpose of this company."

11) "I want to say again that I would love the opportunity to work here." (Presuming that you're still excited about the job as the interview nears its conclusion, you should reiterate your interest and enthusiasm toward the job before you leave the interview. If you want the job, you should make sure they know that you want the job.)

Eight Things You Won't Want to Say in a Job Interview.

Just as there are some things you should definitely try to mention in your interview, there are things that you should not say in an interview. I've listed some common mistakes people make in interviews below. Hopefully, these mistakes will give you an idea of what not to say during an interview.

1) "So, what do you do here?" Someone hasn't done their homework.

2) "I know I don't have much experience, but…" No need to point out your shortcomings and to display a lack of confidence at the same time. If the interviewer has your resume or application, they'll already know that you are short on experience.

3) "I didn't get along with my boss" or "I didn't like the last company I worked for." Trashing past employers is not going to be helpful.

4) "How much vacation time do I get?" This is better discussed in a subsequent

interview when you are discussing salary or the compensation package.

5) "I'd like to start my own business as soon as possible." Why should someone hire you when you're looking to leave as soon as possible.

6) "I'll do whatever you want me to do." Sounds way too desperate.

7) "How soon do you promote employees." Again, this comes across as desperate and will probably make the interviewer think that you can't wait to get past the position they're hiring for.

8) "No, I don't have any questions." I've discussed this previously. If the interviewer asks if you have any questions, don't pass up the opportunity to ask relevant questions. Not only can you use the questions to gain any additional information you're looking for, you'll be able to convey your interest in the position to the interviewer.

10 Soft Skills and How to Demonstrate Them.

When we talk about demonstrating soft skills, I realize that some of you may not know what soft skills are. With this in mind, let me first tell you what soft skills are. Soft skills are personal attributes, personality traits, social cues, or communication abilities. Soft skills are generally a lot less tangible qualities than hard skills. Hard skills are specific job skills or certifications. Examples of hard skills are high school diplomas, college or trade school degrees, professional licenses or certifications, training program completions, on-the-job training, job experience, etc. Hard skills are specific and tangible job skills or proof of job skills. Soft skills are less tangible qualities that are normally not graded by degrees, certificates, or licenses.

When a company is evaluating your resume, they'll generally look first at the hard skills you've listed on your resume. They want to make sure that your hard skills comply with their requirements and also they'll probably want to compare your hard skills with those of the other candidates. For example, if they're looking for an accounting manager, they're generally going to be looking for someone who has an accounting degree and possibly someone who has passed the CPA Board Exam. Those are tangible, hard skills. If you don't have those hard skills, you're likely to be eliminated from the competition.

After these prospective employers have determined your hard skills, they'll then move to your soft skills. If you've "passed" the hard skill requirements, it's likely that whether or not you get the job will be determined by your soft skills. Below I've listed some of the most common soft skills that employers are looking for. As you know, most resumes and cover letters have limited space. Although I encourage you to incorporate your soft skills into your resumes and cover letters, I am aware that there's rarely enough room for you to list all of your soft skills. As a result, it's very important that you mention that you have these skills in your interview. In listing soft skills on your resume, I suggest that you label them as "Transferable Skills", as those are qualities that can usually be transferred to just about any job you're applying for.

For the most part, soft skills are acquired over a period of time instead of in classes or training sessions. Whereas someone can get a journalism major by taking college journalism classes, people generally don't get soft skills such as communication skills, creative skills, or problem-solving skills by taking classes. These soft skills are normally acquired by "learning through experience", or the "school of hard knocks" as some would say.

Soft skills are often considered invaluable by employers, as they are transferable skills that can be used in just about any job. Customer service jobs or jobs in which employees come into direct contact with customers are particularly conducive to soft skills.

In determining which soft skills you want to promote, you should read the posting for that position and you note any soft skills which are mentioned in that posting. These are skills that you should be sure to work into your resume, your cover letter, and your interview, presuming you have the skills they are describing.

For example, if the job posting mentions that the company is looking for someone to become part of their team or the key words in the posting include words such as "team", "teamwork", or "works with others", you'll then know that the company is looking for someone who has this skill. Almost all job postings mention at least a couple of soft skills that the employer is looking for.

Here are some common soft skills which companies are looking for in the people they hire:

1) Motivated or self-motivated.

2) Hard worker or strong work ethic.

3) Adaptability.

4) Team player, able to work well with others.

5) Communicator.

6) Creative thinker, think outside the box, critical thinking.

7) Decision making.

8) Able to resolve conflicts or solve problems.

9) Time management, ability to prioritize.

10) Positivity, enthusiasm.

Again, prior to your interview, you should review the soft skills which are mentioned in the job posting and take an inventory of your own soft skills to see which skills correspond to those that the prospective employer is looking for. Then, you should develop a plan on how you can let the interviewer know you have these skills. For example, if the posting mentions that the employer is looking for a hard worker and you are indeed a hard worker, you'll need to figure out how to drop this into your interview. It won't matter whether you drop this information into the interview directly or indirectly, but you definitely need to let the interview know that you are a hard worker.

If you can provide specific examples to show that you are a hard worker, that's even better. For example, a client of mine was interviewing for a public relations job in which the primary responsibility included events planning. The posting for this job had mentioned that the company was looking to hire someone that was willing to work hard if necessary to complete a project. So, during her interview, my client mentioned that she was a hard worker and she was willing to work whatever hours were necessary to meet the goals of the department or to complete projects on time. She gave the specific example of how she had coordinated a milk carton boat race in one of her previous jobs. (Yes, boats made of milk cartons.) Her company had been the sole sponsor of this event and her supervisor and the management team had underestimated the amount of time it would take to put this even together. As a result, my client and her two team members had to work 12-hour days, 7 days a week in the two weeks prior to the event to make sure that it went off as planned. As a result of the work of her and her team members, the event went off flawlessly and she received plenty of thank you's from company executives who recognized her hard work and a special thank you from the supervisor who had underestimated the amount of time it would take to plan the event.

As you can see, my client not only mentioned that she was a hard worker, she also told a story that showed that she was a hard worker, willing to do whatever was necessary to make the event a success.

I'll give you another example. Another company looking for a customer service representative mentioned that they were looking for candidates who were problem solvers. One of my clients was applying for this job with a promotional products company, a company that provides custom-imprinted items such as t-shirts, pens, tote bags, etc. for corporate customers. My client had previous experience with a promotional products company and he told this story when asked to describe a problem situation in a previous job and how she handled it. A customer had ordered daily calendar refills every year for many years. One year, the customer was delayed in placing their order and by the time my client went to order these calendar refills for her customer, the factory was sold out of them and they were not going to be getting more of these refills, as they were made in Malaysia and the delivery time to receive additional refill pads was going to be well into March or April of the upcoming year. Instead of just dropping this problem back into her customer's lap, my client worked immediately to find another factory that had similar, but not identical, refills that would work. She had to do about three hours of research and make about a dozen phone calls to come up with a solution to the problem, but she did. She then contacted her customer to make them aware of the initial problem and, at the same time, explain that she had found a solution. She immediately offered to send the customer a photo of the alternate calendar refill pads and the customer found them to be acceptable.All of this for a customer who was placing a small order of about $150.

This story certainly showed my client's ability to attack a problem and solve it, despite the small size of the order. It shows that she was able to go "above and beyond" to solve a problem on behalf of her customer.

If you can find a way to effectively communicate your soft skills to your interviewer, you'll give yourself a much better chance to land the job.

**Chapter 14: The Next Step**

To begin with, make the "Fit Test"

Be totally clear for yourself that the part and organization you'd like to request truly fits with your abilities, profession track, proficient and individual goals, convictions and encounters. Alternately check, on the off chance that you may coordinate with the way of life and needs of the organization you'd like to join. In the event that there's no apparent fit as of now in this first step, don't proceed onward and don't squander your or any other individual's chance by needing to lead a meeting. Just in the event that you think about, and have confidence in, and feel about such a "fit," you can and you will have - and thusly emanate - a 100% inspiration level towards the new part and the new organization. What's more, that is the thing that it takes to succeed. Each great questioner will acknowledge rapidly how energetic you are about her organization and how energized you are about the offered position.

Research the Target Company

To be all around arranged is a large portion of the triumph. Still, I'm shocked what number of competitors would touch base at meetings, notwithstanding for senior level positions, and not having contemplated our qualities, statement of purpose, initiative standards, items, and so on. Why might they have not inspected our Internet webpage, not read our most recent press discharges, why might they have no clue about what our rivals are doing, what our present and future difficulties could resemble? Try not to misunderstand me: It's not about being or turning into a specialist about the organization and part being referred to. It's all the more about having gained a sound learning before the meeting to be capable defining your own, insight based sentiment which you'll have to express at the interview(s).

Know your interviewer(s)

Today it's less demanding than at any other time in recent memory to gather data about your questioners. Burn through 40-50 minutes on Google, LinkedIn, and so forth and you ought to be clear about titles, parts, vocations, and so on about the considerable number of individuals who'll meeting you. If not, solicit the individual who's dependable from arranging the meetings and/or with whom you're in contact to give you some foundation data about the individuals you'll meet. Tending to questioners with their names and verifiably (or expressly without overstating) revealing to them that you know (a smidgen) about their professions, accomplishments, and so forth is neighborly, as well as shows regard and hobby. You'd be astonished to hear how adversely it is seen by numerous questioners, in the event that you don't have the foggiest idea about these things. Also, unexpectedly, how complimented huge numbers of them will be, on the off chance that you are mindful of a few truths and achievements of their expert lives. It's similar to, all things considered!

Land On-Time and Professionally Focused

It's never a decent begin, if an applicant arrives late taking into account her or his own flaw (e.g. having taken the wrong prepare, not having thought seriously about substantial movement at a certain time, not having discovered the right passage of the building, and so on.). If there should be an occurrence of uncertainty and on the off chance that you live further far from the venue of the meeting, you ought to consider arriving the prior night and staying at lodging. Great executives won't just repay related costs, yet will likewise admire your keenness and expert state of mind. It's a given that a crisp personality is a considerably more engaged and a significantly more certain one. What's more, leading an effective meeting is firmly connected with possessing and showing a solid level of self-assurance.

## 11. Confirm Your Appearance, Style and Tone

Imagine you're wearing a short-sleeved shirt, no tie and an easy going pair of trousers when meeting for a prospective employee meet-up to one of the nation's top insurance agencies? Alternately, envision – for entertainment purposes - you took out your most loved Bryony matching suit for a meeting with the originator and CEO of the most sultry Internet start-up around (who is one of those Harvard drop-outs and who is in no way, shape or form intrigued by any grown-up toys). Past these more clear things like appearance and dress, you ought to additionally pay consideration on the vocabulary you're utilizing. You ought to use words and expressions which are common in the objective organization, its businesses, and its industry. Likewise when applying e.g. for a position as a trademark attorney, you may need to appear to be not kidding and mindful. While when going for a business or promoting position, you should be arranged demonstrating attributes of essentialness, drive, and stamina (among others). At last, be mindful of the early introduction you pass on when meeting for the first run through the interviewer(s). It numbers and it will be recalled – deliberately and sub-intentionally - for quite a while. In the event that you were somebody who grinned a ton, on the off chance that you had a firm hand-shake, a wonderful and clear voice and on the off chance that you had searched for eye-contact amid the snippet of making the colleague with the questioner. Essential to comment that the procedure of "making the early introduction" regularly as of now begins even before the meeting; e.g. when you meet the assistant, a partner of the questioner, or somebody offering you a beverage, and so forth. The "impact" of such aberrant partners is the more grounded, the littler the organization you're applying with.

*Know yourself and The Value You Might be Adding*

Before entering any meeting circle you would need to verify that you know your qualities and your ranges for development. Be practical and legitimate about them. Have the capacity to rundown and to clarify them by utilizing concrete and short samples and explain what you mean when e.g. you were to express that "you are eager and constantly need to tempest ahead by grabbing every single recognized opportunities." You ought to have an unmistakable seeing about what is searched for at your objective organization and the employment you're requisitioning. You should be capable clarifying why you accept that you're the one "meriting" the occupation by producing most esteem to the organization.

*Suspect Questions and Possible Areas of Concern*

Good questioners will attempt to envision you being on the part they're meeting for.

How would they isn't that right? Really simple! They attempt to match your qualities, your encounters, illustrations given by you, the way you talk and act with their way of life, their business and administration standards, and with the necessities of the part they're selecting for. Sample: If you request head of bookkeeping with an organization which prides itself of rearing chiefs who prepare to stun the world and long haul, you would need to think of maybe a couple cases when you proved being not just numbers and point of interest concentrated in your past vocation, however when you likewise went about as a visionary and a comprehensive scholar. Record conceivable inquiries, form replies, and even practice in any event some of them with a companion, friend, and so forth. Saying that, stay adaptable amid the meeting and don't attempt to answer with rethought and reformulated responses to all inquiries.

Stay Open-Minded, Positive, And Always Engaged: Regardless of how the meeting goes – or what you think how it goes (as these two are regularly unique), your levelheadedness ought to show interest, engagement, and well disposed receptiveness. Consider the meeting as a chance to learn and to develop. Notwithstanding the result, whilst focusing and making inquiries, obviously, you are permitted to grin. During all this you need take care of your non-verbal communication. Correspondence frequently is about what is said, as well as for the most part about how something is communicated – verbally and non-verbally. In this admiration, you ought not to think about the meeting as a type of restricted correspondence, i.e. just you clarifying and noting inquiries. Try not to miss the chance to build up a dialog on a level playing field with the questioner. In the event that you are interested about something, in the event that you didn't see well an announcement, on the off chance that you'd like to get more clarifications on a vital subject, then you have to pose your questions. It's what each accomplished questioner would anticipate from you: You just escape from the meeting, what you are willing to put into it.

Act naturally and Do Not Pretend

You ought not to take a stab at being everybody's dear or imagining being another person just to land the position neither in life nor a meeting.

Certainly, as said beforehand, you would need to adjust and to demonstrate that you comprehended what the organization, the part, and the meeting is about. Saying that, never surrender effectively your centre qualities and feelings. Be prepared to enter a decent and usefully drove talk with diverse purpose of perspectives. Imperative to recognize, nonetheless, to stay tolerant, receptive and to talk about in an empathic and reality based way. Forget feelings, governmental issues, and any compelling musings and positions. One last remark: Even in the wake of having done an exhaustive examination of the organization and the part you're keen on, it may turn out in the meeting that some central perspectives are not in-accordance with your desires or, and that likewise may happen, the position itself does not appear to fit any more. Once – and after great reflection – this ought to end up clear to you then you ought not go for the part nor acknowledge it, on the off chance that it was advertised. Probably it would be an agonizing background and it would not work out.

Complete the Interview in Style

 The last piece of a decent meeting more often than not begins with the applicant asking some brilliant last inquiries. Case in point addresses about the more general system of the organization, about what the questioner considers as being significant for being fruitful at work (if not secured already), or – if illumination is required – about the part and its specifics. In any case, you ought to have recorded a rundown of both more nonspecific and more particular inquiries. Three to four are adequate (If there were still all the more on your rundown towards the end of the meeting, this may show that you were not effectively enough making inquiries in the meeting until this purpose of time). It is crucial not asking your questions in a manner as being perceived as feeling obligated having to ask them. Instead they should be presented in an engaged way and you should be prepared to follow-upon on answers which might not be precise enough, or not having the depth you would have expected. You need to take care that all of your relevant questions will be answered during the interview. That is your right and obligation towards yourself. If not, you might lack important information and you might join the wrong company. At the very end of the interview ask about next steps of the interview process. Personally, I also appreciate candidates who ask for a very first assessment at the end of the interview. Most important, however, and regardless of how the interview went, it is crucial to express your gratitude for the interview and to politely say goodbye.

## Two More Things Many Candidates forget About

Firstly, nothing wrong with, if you send to the interviewers – or at least to the principal interviewer – a short mail after the interview and thanking again for the interviews and mentioning that you would be looking forward to receiving their answer. This should be done, however, in a short and non-hyperbolized manner. Secondly, and this is very relevant in case you had not gotten the job, you should contact the company to ask for a personal and detailed feedback of your interview and about your performance. This is very helpful in order to improve for the next interview. In addition, you should reflect on the previous interview(s) and go through it step by step. Reviewing what went well and not so well. Focus on the improvement areas and write down specific action steps on how to better prepare and execute in the future.

Bonus Chapter

More Tips and Tricks

•As you are about to enter the interview room take 2 or 3 deep breaths to calm your nerves. You will do better if you are relaxed and have a calm mind.

•Your preparation for the job interview should be taken seriously. The competition against another candidate with a better qualification is fierce. Preparation helps you keep what's in your mind, and not slip it when you're in a most uncomfortable position. An interview is the key before a company hires you, so you better discover how to sell yourself before meeting with the prospective employer.

•Don't be afraid to be confident. Set your mind to why you are the best candidate for the job. If you truly feel that way, it's likely you'll pass the sentiment on to your interviewer.

•When you are introduced to the panel of interviewers, shake hands firmly with each person, create eye contact with each person & say that you are pleased to meet them, and smile as you say so.

- Don't say something you'll regret later. Think before you speak.

- If the venue is far from your place of residence, stop in the washroom when you arrive to reset your hair, tie, etc.

- Don't play with your chair while waiting to be called.

- Start preparing for the interview well before the interview day. Thorough preparation is a prerequisite to success in any interview. Ideally, start preparing about a month before the interview. If that isn't possible, start preparing as soon as you are able.

- Don't munch on junk food while waiting for the interview. You wouldn't want to offer a crumb-covered or sticky hand to the interviewer.

## Chapter 15: Why Do You Want This Job?

This question also seems like a throw away but it is a question very often asked in an interview. Of course the main reason anyone wants any job is for money but the employer is searching for your true interest level. Just as in the previous chapter the employer would like to find someone who is truly invested in the line of work for which they are interviewing. Someone who is passionate is more likely to remain in the position longer and will take the job more seriously. Those who have a personal passion are more likely to bring about positive change and work ethic and these are things an employer will see as an asset.

When asked this question begin your response with how and where you found the position. What about the job first snagged your attention and made you decide it was a job you had to apply for? Refer to specific wording in the job listing which stood out to you or aspects of the job which made you feel you would be a good fit with elongated interest in investing your time in working with the company.

After you have begun your answer this way you can ask questions you already know the answers to and explain then how those answers fit into your personal goals and passions for the position. Within those responses you can then explain how those answers make the job even more interesting and rewarding to you in your job, and if possible, your personal life as well.

Focus your response in explaining how the job matches what you are looking for as a career path and the growth within that path. Specify that you are drawn to the mission of the company and believe in the same core values such as X,Y,Z. You will want to do your research and find out the core values of the company and find ones which match your own personal beliefs. Explaining that you feel you can provide a lot of value to the company due to your experience and expertise and are looking forward to all you can learn from the position and are excited to undergo the growth process.

You can also talk about how you are strongly motivated by the core values of the company and strive for similar points not only in your career but your personal life outside of work. When discussing the details, you can emphasis the portions of the work you would be excited to perform and how you are drawn to that type of work with excitement and purpose. When companies know the person they have hired is fulfilling a life's purpose they feel they have hired someone who will be a longstanding asset to the company.

Furthermore, you can mention how you think you would be a great fit for the role because of what you have learned about the company. If you feel you are a natural fit for the role in question and that the job does not only fulfill needs for the company but needs for you as an employee. The desire to be a willing participant and contributor to the forward motion of the company will be a deciding factor in who the company decides to hire in the role.

Having done your research on the company and knowing what the company is known for, the industry it supports, where the company is based, and how many employees the company has, will help you in your discussion. Statements which vocalize that the company is an attractive place for people with your skills and talents to work because of the companies ability to utilize their employees skills and talents for the betterment of the business will help you show your deep ties to the type of work for which you are applying.

Within your response avoid saying negative things about previous positions, companies, or employees. Someone who is willing to be negative in a job interview is likely to be negative on the job and will bring with them negativity which can rub off on other employees. Potential employers are looking for people who will uplift moral and not bring it down.

Furthermore, avoid speaking about previous positions as being too easy or too difficult. Anything which can make your previous positions seem trivial, or as a burden, will ultimately label you as someone who is not fully invested in the job and has a more self centered attitude. It is better to focus your energy on ensuring you show you take the job at hand very seriously.

WHAT ARE YOUR INTERESTS?

Employers are always wanting employees who have a well-rounded skill set and experience background. Some positions focus on some factors which may be more desirable to an employee than others or some companies may have a separate position for those aspects completely. When asked this question the employer is once again checking to see how much the position will really hold your interest. They ask these types of questions to weed out potential employees who would be more satisfied with positions which are better suited for skills and experience which holds their interest.

When answering this question you should focus on what initially drove you to this type of work. What first sparked your interest in the field of study or work gaining experience? Was there something in your life which made the type of work extremely rewarding or perhaps there is a life's passion and need to be in a job which allows you certain intrinsic rewards the position provides? Focus on how the job you desire is the position for which you have been working towards and would love nothing more than to help the company succeed.

When answering these types of questions it is always beneficial to respond in ways which show a group centered mentality. The purpose of you being hired is to help the overall success of the company and the mission not for your own personal financial gain. Group centered mentalities demonstrate a work ethic which is less likely to make self centered decisions and ultimately will be the best for a company. Those who work more for their own gain are less likely able to work well in groups and follow instructions.

Avoid telling long stories or going off on tangents when responding. Keep your answers precise and to the point. Keeping answers short and simple will also keep the attention of your interviewer and keep their interest longer. It will also demonstrate an ability to keep information detailed but concise.

WHAT ARE YOUR STRENGTHS IN A TEAM?

Employers who are asking this question are doing so because their employees will often be expected to work as a team. Many companies today are set up for success by working in small groups and even viewing the entire company as one large team. If an employee is unable to work well in a team mentality they may not be best suited for this type of company set up.

When responding it is best to focus on what attributes and skills you can provide which can help a team set up and have helped in the past. Talk specifically about a time when you had worked in a team before and what your specific roll was within that team. Stating specifics will aid you in being detailed without taking too much time and will also allow your employer know you have actually worked within a team.

Being specific enough to detail which exact position and whom the supervisor was will allow your potential employer to make contact with whomever was involved should they desire more details. It is also a good idea to remain as positive as possible, give praise to other members of the team, and specify how each of your contributions was helpful when using them together. This shows your potential employer that you give credit where credit is due and do not see yourself as the only contributor in a group setting.

Even if your experience was that you pulled all of the weight, it is better to always provide a positive attitude towards any situation. Chose your wording carefully and be kind towards those who were assigned to the team. Talk about what you enjoyed about working with a team and how it helped you grow.

When talking about your strengths state the things you are proud of and what you have worked on. You can also go into a little detail on how you have worked to become better in the areas you now consider a strength. Focus on your goals and how your strengths are helping you gain your footing to get closer to achieving them. You can also discuss what strengths you have which help in a team which may have been learned or strengthened on the job or through the mentorship of another employee or supervisor. Explaining what things motivate you to work hard within a group is also helpful.

Avoid speaking negatively about a project, the group, a particular person, or the company in question. Once again this will only alert your potential employer to the possibility of you being a negative influence. It is always better to remain positive and speak kindly about every situation, even those which may have been less than optimal.

Also avoid speaking as though you were the only contributor in a group. Even if this were true a potential employer could take this as a sign of being self-centered. Employers like to work with those who are willing and able to work in a group setting. People who spend their time talking about the lack of ability from those in their team will likely be ones who are quick to complain and cause friction within a group.

Instead of talking about what aspects of the group setting were poor, or explaining why you would work better alone, do your best to talk about how working in a group ultimately helps move the entire team of the all encompassing company forward towards its goals. You may also speak towards the exemplary abilities of each person bringing their talents to the team. Doing this will show you are humble in your own abilities as well and that you are willing to give energy and effort towards another person's success.

When potential employees show they are willing to put their own personal goals aside to help a team member, or the team as a whole, shine brightly, the potential employer will see this not as a sign of weakness but as a sign that you are a true team player. The overall success matters more than the gold star attached to your personal name. Companies like to see people who are not out for their own fame and glory.

People who only desire to ensure their name is always placed in positions of honor are at risk for being opportunistic. Opportunistic behavior doesn't help the team but only puts the person in question at the forefront and being the center of attention. While this can be helpful in cases where a person is working solo, while in a team set up, this type of behavior is viewed as obnoxious or even as a hindrance towards the group goal.

WHAT ARE YOUR WEAKNESSES IN A TEAM?

Employers asking this question usually ask what your strengths are first and then your weaknesses second. Their reason for doing so is to double check your own answers and dig a little deeper to see if you are really only speaking positively of your team because you are hiding something, or if you see yourself as overly talented. You could also lack confidence. Employers are looking for a well rounded person who understands fully their own strengths and weaknesses and knows how to work around them to make the team ultimately function in the best way possible.

Rather than talking negatively about yourself and being demeaning it is best to focus on the strengths of the people who were in the team with you. Talk about how the leader led and what they brought to the table and what you learned from their leadership. Talk about the stand out contributors and what you learned from working with them.

Bring emphasis to how happy you are for the success of the people in the team and what they brought to the mix. From there talk about how you helped that person with their success. This way the weakness is really a strength because you are able to help others shine and work together rather than focusing on being a complete failure. Again, approaching negative questions with a positive voice is usually a more impactful tactic than simply answering with a negative.

Talking about the steps you are taking to improve your weaknesses will show a maturity and growth potential. Talking about areas where you would like to grow as well such as programs or leadership tactics you would like to learn which will help you with your career path down the line will be an incising incentive to the company. You can demonstrate the potential opportunity with you by giving an example of something you were poor at and worked towards being better and how that has overall impacted your job performance.

Avoid at all costs talking about complete failure for yourself or the team, in portions, or a whole. Responding as though your entire task was a failure, or that you yourself were a failure, is only going to shine more on the negative than any positive you have previously answered in other questions. Do your best to steer the conversation towards the positive to keep your interview upbeat.

Should you veer towards speaking ill of projects, persons, the team, or the company there is a good chance this negativity will weigh stronger in your overall interview than any positive you have put forth. There is also a chance that you could paint yourself as a negative person who simply does not fit well with a team mentality or structure when in reality you may have only had a rift with a few specifics of the team dynamic or set up.

## Chapter 16: During The Interview: Common Questions Part 1

Interview questions can be broken down into a handful of common types: credential and experience verification questions; opinion and behavioral questions; competency questions; brainteasers or other nonsense questions are the most frequent types of questions that are brought up in a typical interview situation. While perhaps the most important of these are an opinion and behavioral questions, we will start here with issues that deal with credentials and experience, as they are among the first questions that you will field at an interview. Knowing how to talk about your credentials, qualifications, experience, and other elements of your character is crucial to presenting yourself as the best candidate for the job.

Credential verification questions can do a couple of things in the course of an interview: first, they can allow for a breaking of the ice at the beginning, in order to allow both interviewer and candidate to warm up to the process; second, they can serve as a jumping-off point to elaborate on particular achievements in your educational or work history that will illustrate your fittingness for the job; third, they can give you the opportunity to explain away any gaps or unconventional issues with your resume.

First, credential questions can be a way to ease into the interview, allowing for everybody to settle in and relax a bit. Because these kinds of questions essentially ask you to review and verify your resume, be sure that you have a copy quick at hand in case you need to quickly look at something. Otherwise, you should be able to readily answer these kinds of questions without hesitation. The interviewer may ask a series of verification questions or just one or two that he or she is interested in; partly, this depends on how detailed your resume is in the first place. If certain credentials are of greater interest to your potential employer, then this serves as a way into broader issues, as follows.

Second, certain credentials might encourage interviewers to ask some follow up questions: for example, they might be interested in knowing why you stayed for so long (or so short) at a particular place of employment; or, they might be interested in knowing how certain kinds of coursework were relevant to your overall educational achievement. They might also use credential questions to prompt you to show a link between various activities and interests you've engaged with in the past: that is, you might be encouraged to show how seemingly disparate parts of your overall credential portfolio actually link together. Say you've been working as a graphic designer, and you also list that you volunteered at a food pantry: these credentials don't necessarily seem to have anything to do with one another. You should be prepared to show how you have learned skills from each that complement the other. Additionally, credential verification questions could lead to the interviewer following up on how these past credentials might serve the current position for which you are applying. That is, you might be asked not only how your credentials have reinforced your growing skillset through past experience but also how these credentials link to the requirements being asked of you for the current job.

Third, when an interviewer asks credential verification questions, he or she might be giving you the opportunity to explain or justify particular gaps in your resume. For example, if there is a gap in employment, then the interviewer might ask you what you were doing during that time and why the gap exists in the first place. In this case, be very prepared to answer honestly and thoroughly. For another example, the gap in your resume might be related to a particular set of skills. An interviewer can use a credential verification question to prompt you to expand on the kind of soft skills—leadership, effective communication, conflict resolution—needed to fulfill the requirements of a particular position. It can also be a prompt for you to expand upon a specific promotion or project. Finally, when reviewing your resume, an interviewer might candidly ask why certain skills seem to be missing. Be prepared to explain this, as well, and demonstrate how you intend to develop this skill or fill in your resume's gaps.

Beyond those opportunities, credential verification questions are also closely related to qualification questions. In this case, you are being asked to expand upon how your credentials and experience make you qualified for the position at hand. Your credentials reveal your qualifications in a concise and concrete way; however, the qualifications you possess represent more than mere credentials but also general work and life experience, in addition to the possession of a variety of soft skills that will assist you with any position you might want to tackle.

Some experience verification questions will simply ask you what particular, and concrete tasks did you perform during your past workplace situation. This might be something like "on your resume, you mention that you participated in Project X. What were you responsible for contributing?" This is an example of why it is so important for you to review your resume and have a clear sense of how you might explain each individual job position, task, or other events on it. These questions give you the opportunity to demonstrate that the variety of skills necessary to work on concrete tasks is valuable skills to any position to which you might be applying.

Experience verification questions also give you the opportunity to talk about past accomplishments, whether they be in the form of increased production and/or revenue, promotions, awards, or unique opportunities that you were able to take advantage of because of your exceptional previous performance. Oftentimes, an interviewer will simply ask you what your greatest accomplishments at a particular job or other experience might be. One effective way to prepare for an interview, in general, would be to keep a copy of your resume, wherein you take notes about particular talking points for each element of the resume: you may not necessarily have the space to list every accomplishment from every position, of course, but if you jot down notes about interesting accomplishments, the interview gives you the space during which to talk about a wider variety of successes than your resume can reveal. For example, if you worked on a particular project that received a significant amount of external attention and you were asked to speak to the media about it, this is an accomplishment that may not merit being listed on your resume but is certainly legitimate and strong enough to discuss in an interview. It reveals not only your expertise and dedication to a particular project but also your effective communication skills and flexibility to perform duties beyond the specific tasks required for production.

Another kind of experience verification question will ask how you handle difficult situations, in particular how you previously handled conflict resolution issues. Conflict resolution is one of those crucial soft skills that employers are looking for, especially in industries that prize teamwork and cross-departmental cooperation. Demonstrating that you have the ability to work with a diverse group of people, with varied skillsets and personality attributes, reveals that you are a valuable asset beyond the actual hard skills that you have been educated or trained to perform. Conflict resolution questions ask that you show a variety of attributes that allow you to resolve issues as they arise, including mediation, empathy, facilitation, creative problem-solving, and accountability. There are even entire positions within organizations that are dedicated to conflict resolution capabilities, but this is a valuable skill for any employee. Be sure to identify, prior to the interview, a particular instance at a specific job wherein you were called upon—or, better yet, simply took up the responsibility without being expressly asked—to resolve conflicts between staff members or between co-workers and management. Showing that you can handle conflict with poise and thoughtfulness reveals a lot about your worth as an employee overall. It also reflects your ability to understand and navigate a complex situation without creating more conflict. Be especially careful not to assign blame to others or to otherwise project negativity; focus on the attributes that you have, as well as the concrete actions you undertook, in order to resolve a difficult matter during previous work experience.

These are just a few of the kinds of credential, qualification, or experience questions you might be asked to relay during an interview: others might address what you consider to be challenging (this can allow you to speak to potential gaps in credentials or skills) or press you to justify how your experience and qualifications will impact the company's productivity and bottom line.

**Chapter 17: The Phone Rings**

We are experiencing a period in time that unemployment rate is reaching 48% in some countries of EU and significant unemployment rates exists in USA and Asia region of the world. That percentage of unemployment does not make it easy for anyone to get their chance to a new or a better job.

So you have just finished college or you have been unemployed the last few months or simply looking for a job that will boost your career. Regardless on which of the above mentioned positions you belong to you have done your research and already send out a few resumes to a variety of companies for positions that you are interested in.

Some of these resumes might get rejected and some of them never got an answer back. You have decided to send few more as the days passed by.

On your way home from the supermarket on a Tuesday afternoon your phone rings. When you answer the phone you hear the following: "Good afternoon Sir. My name is Maria and I am calling on behalf of the head of the IT department of the Software Company you have applied for few days back. We would like to schedule an interview with you on Thursday morning at 10am at our central offices". Although you might be over excited as you have been waiting for this call with anxiety the last few days or even weeks remain as calm as possible and make sure that the below are clear to you:

• You have a clear understanding on which company is the one you have received a phone call from. When sending out a number of resumes it could happen that you have confused the company names. If for any reason you are not sure ask again in a polite manner such as " Excuse me Madam, Can you please repeat your name and information as am driving at the moment and there is a lot of background noise? "

• Place a note and a reminder on the upcoming interview including the information below:

1. The name of the person that have contacted you to schedule this appointment.

2. The name of the head of the department that you will be doing the interview with.

3. The name of the company.

4. The date and time of the interview.

5.The location of the interview.

6.Any requested documents such as copy of your resume or possible references.

•Make sure that you keep the phone conversation short and pleasant. Ask only the necessary information required for the interview and keep smiling during the conversation. Smiling shows and conveys positive energy and confidence and this is something that all employers are looking for to bring in to their teams. Recent research completed shows that smile can be "felt" and transmitted to the person you are having the phone conversation with. But at the same time be careful not to overdo it.

•Be professional. Choose the right words. During this short phone conversation to arrange your interview you are in a way being evaluated from the company. This will be your first evaluation from the PA of the head of department. You never know who has an influence in the company and the position which you are applying for so treat everyone as they have equal power.

## Conclusion

I hope this book was able to help you find clarity regarding successfully getting through job interviews. As you must have realized by now, the only way to convince your potential employers about your skills is first to be convinced about them yourself. You need to let yourself believe that you are truly deserving of the job that you are applying for in order to communicate the same conviction to your interviewer.

The fact is, we are living in extremely competitive times. The job market is getting tougher to crack into with each passing day. A glorious degree from a fancy school would just not make the cut. The company will assess your employability based on multiple factors. Your skills and experience are important. But what is all the more important for them is to understand whether you'd settle well within the company's culture. This book has equipped you with all the right tools at your arsenal to ace a job interview. The next step is to find a job that you are truly passionate about pursuing and find a company culture that resonates with your beliefs and values. A little research and preparedness can help you get an edge over fellow applicants and answer the interviewers' queries confidently and with passion. We hope this book helped you find the clarity and direction you were looking for to land your desired job. All the best!

www.ingramcontent.com/pod-product-compliance
Lightning Source LLC
Chambersburg PA
CBHW072013070526
44583CB00015B/1465